Along the Garden Path
Garden Related Activities, Quizzes, Stories & Trivia
by Hank Bruce & Tomi Jill Folk

Petals & Pages Press
Rio Rancho, New Mexico

Other books by Hank Bruce & Tomi Jill Folk

by Hank Bruce & Tomi Jill Folk
Global Gardening
The Family Caregiver's Journal: A Guide to Facing the Terminal Illness of a Loved One
Gardening Projects for Horticultural Therapy Programs
Garden Projects for the Classroom and Special Learning Programs
The Abundant Harvest Garden for The American Southwest
Windowsill Whimsy, Gardening & Horticultural Therapy Projects for Small Spaces
Seniors Illustrated Vol. 1
Seniors Illustrated Vol. 2

by Tomi Jill Folk
Visits with the Old Indian Storyteller

by Hank Bruce
Peace Beyond All Fear, a Tribute to John Denver's Vision
Oblivion, a Novel Place to Live
Gardens for the Senses, Gardening as Therapy
Yankee's Guide to Florida Gardening
Uncommon Scents, Growing Herbs & Spices in Florida
The Pocket Library of Florida Gardening (4 volumes)
Where Do Snowmen Go When They Melt?
The Courage to Create: A Writer's Workbook
Nelson's Guide to Florida Roses
Gardening Trivia

Along the Garden Path
Garden Related Activities, Quizzes, Stories & Trivia
by Hank Bruce & Tomi Jill Folk

Published by Petals & Pages Press © 2009
ISBN 978-0-9797057-5-5

Petals & Pages Press
860 Polaris Blvd SE
Rio Rancho, NM 87124
www.petalsandpagespress.com
petals_pages@msn.com

Acknowledgments:
A book like this doesn't just happen. Years of on-the-job experiences, both successes and failures went into what's between these covers. We are very appreciative of the advice, input, suggestions and inspiration provided by elders and activity professionals from across the United States. Thank you all for being a part of this effort. A special thanks to all those who participated in these activities as a part of horticultural therapy programs we conducted in so many senior communities around the United States over the past thirty years. Thanks also to Paris Saizan for the Fruitcake poem on page 11.

Dedicated to Joyce Folk

Who harvested many vegetables to feed our family,
and countless fragrant & beautiful flowers to nourish the spirit.
Thanks Mom

Along the Garden Path
table of contents

Introduction

This is a collection of over 50 diverse plant related activities, gardening without getting your hands dirty, planting ideas that may need nurturing, but don't have to be watered. These activities are designed to serve as conversation topics, memory triggers, and perhaps spark a few ideas along the way. There are a few gardening suggestions and a healthy crop of good humor to harvest.

This book is a journey down the garden path from yesterday into tomorrow. It was written for activity and horticultural therapy programs in senior communities and private homes. Families and friends can enjoy strolling through these pages, pausing to smell the flowers, harvesting a few veggies and perhaps pulling a few weeds along the way. Like a real garden there are surprises, discoveries to be made, ideas to be discussed, and opinions to be voiced.

The quizzes are diverse in format and subject, just like an old fashioned garden. There are many opportunities to smile, chuckle or even laugh out loud. That's ok, we planned it that way. We wanted this to be a sensory experience and this is your sense of humor being exercised. We also want those who enter these pages to set free their sense of adventure, be brave, courageous and bold.

When you don't know the answer, guess, speak up, share your memories and your dreams. Many of these quizzes and activities are designed to be done as a group or a family, with everyone making a contribution. There are no time limits on any of these because each of these can take us down a garden path less traveled. Once the mind is opened and the conversations begin you never know where they will lead. For many of these quizzes, like life itself, there are no "right" answers, only an opportunity to share individual thoughts, ideas and experiences.

Everyone has the opportunity to create their own personal bouquet of smiles, friendship, delightful memories recalled and creative new ideas discovered. Many of these activities and quizzes provide an opportunity to share, enlighten, and engage. The quiz is only the beginning, the first step along the garden path. The next step is up to you; it's your decision. Don't be timid.

- Try your hand at the Vegetable Soup Game, going through the alphabet pulling related items from your memories.
- Join the world famous plant detective, Sherlock Humus, who bears a slight resemblance to Sir Arthus Conan Doyle's fictional character, as he solves an assortment of plant mysteries.
- You are free to burst into song as you engage the musical quizzes.
- Separate fact from fiction, and myth from reality, in some of these quizzes.
- You get to create a perfect salad and provide the punch lines for garden jokes.
- Enjoy the conversation suggestions and the activities that accompany many of these little mental exercises.
- Have the courage to create some of your own.
- Enjoy the little stories and share a few of your own.

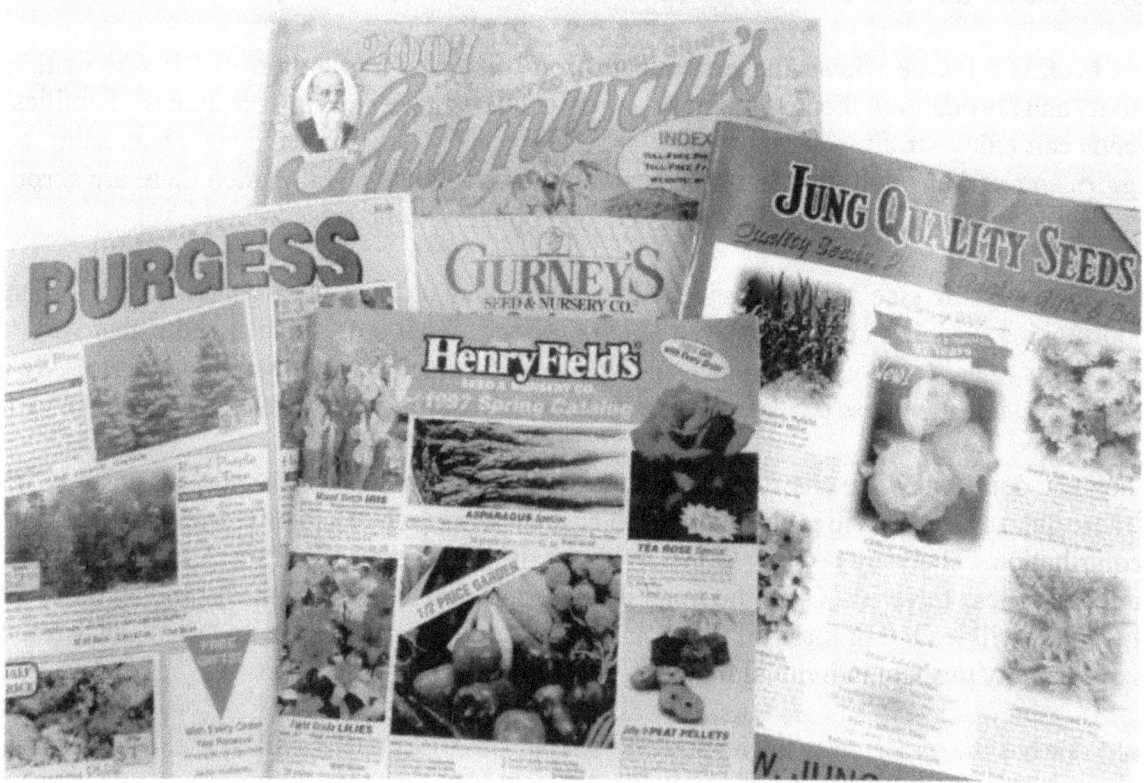

What Would the New Year Be Without All Those Seed Catalogs in the Mailbox?

"As I write, snow is falling outside my Maine window, and indoors all around me half a hundred garden catalogues are in bloom."
Katharine S. White

Vern was a garden addict. Christmas was only a diversion while he waited for the Henry Fields, Gurney's, Burpee's and a multitude of other catalogs to begin arriving. A check from Publisher's Clearing House could have been in the day's mail, but he would have passed it up to rip open the new Shumway's offering of proven vegetables and old fashioned flowers.

He would spread them out on the kitchen table and study them as if he were cramming for a college final. He could look out the window at a winter landscape covered with snow, but he would see rows of sweet corn, morning glories climbing the arbor, and tomatoes ripening on the vine.

Almost every winter afternoon Vern, with an armload of his mail order seed catalogs, could be found at the senior meals site. This was an opportunity to talk gardening with his friends, fellow diners and strangers. The following little quiz is adapted from one Vern created to test the gardening knowledge of his friends. This one is easy. Some of his other quizzes prompted unprintable comments.

Oh, one last observation before you begin. Vern always encouraged everyone to think of this as an "open book test." They were free to use the catalogs on the table to find the answers. It was even ok to talk and ask each other's opinion. Often they would get sidetracked and never get the quiz finished. That's ok too.

Think Spring Seed Catalog Quiz

1. A TRADE PACK is **larger** or **smaller** than the regular offering?

2. An ounce of tomato seeds is approximately how many seeds according the R. H. Shumway?
a) 75   b) 150   c) 500   d) 1000

3. Baby onion plants are called
a) greens   b) starters   c) sets   d) eyes

4. Squash are usually classified as
a) summer or winter   b) raw or cooked   c) soft or solid skin

5. The typical garden peas that we shell and serve with carrots are also known as
a) sweet peas   b) pole peas   c) English peas   d) split peas

6. Parks Whopper is a large tomato first introduced by which seed company?
a) Burger King   b) Parks   c) Jung   d) Henry Field

7. Spaghetti Squash is really a
a) myth   b) squash   c) stringy parasite that grows on Zucchini

8. Heirloom vegetables are
a) exotic hybrids   b) Old-Fashioned varieties   c) Grown in historic gardens

9. Pumpkins are most closely related to
a) squash   b) cucumbers   c) cantaloupe   d) gourds

10. Varieties of vegetables that you can save the seeds from, and when planted next year will grow and bear the same fruit or vegetable are called
a) hybrids   b) true to name   c) open pollinated   d) antique

Answers: 1 larger, 2-c, 3-c, 4-a, 5-c, 6-b, 7-b, 8-b, 9-a, 10-c

What's That Growing in your Garden?

For the rest of these Vern listed three varieties and his "victims" had to match these with the vegetable on the right. (*Note: Some veggies are used more than once.*)

1. __Early Jersey Wakefield, Copenhagen & Flat Dutch   A. Beets

2. __Summer Crookneck, Patty Pan & Acorn   B. Green Beans

3. __Early Alaska, Little Marvel & Wando   C. Cabbage

4. __Silver Queen, Golden Jubilee & Country Gentleman   D. Carrots

5. __Box Car Willie, Beefsteak, Big Boy   E. Sweet Corn

6. __Black Diamond, Charleston Grey, Sugar Baby   F. Lettuce

7. __Kennebec, Russet & Yukon Gold   G. Peas

8. __Blue Hubbard, Zucchini & Butternut   H. Potatoes

9. __Danvers Half Long, Coreless Nantes & Imperator   I. Squash

10. __Black Seeded Simpson, Oak Leaf & Romaine   J. Tomatoes

11. __Abraham Lincoln, Homestead & Cherry   K. Watermelon

12. __Blue Lake, Kentucky Wonder & Contender

13. __Bountiful, Tender Crop & Hurricane

14. __Butter Head, Iceberg & Ruby leaf

15. __Bull's Blood, Detroit Dark Red & Cylindra

Answers: 1-C, 2-I, 3-G, 4-E, 5-J, 6-K, 7-H, 8-I, 9-D, 10-F, 11-J, 12-B, 13-B, 14-F, 15-A

But the Open Book Test was only the beginning.

Vern had everyone using these old seed catalogs in all sorts of creative ways. He started "The Gray Power Tomato Club" and each week the winner was awarded either a tomato plant, a ripe tomato, or one of his niece's special tomato recipe home canned delights.

This all started innocently enough when one of the other diners got bored with the "test" and started cutting pictures out of the nearest catalog. She arranged them to make an absolutely absurd farmer's face. Vern issued the challenge to all present to return tomorrow with their own creation. These were taped up on the wall and the other visitors to the site voted on the ugliest "work of art."

Olivia started her Gardener's Journal by clipping photos from the catalogs and putting them on the page where she kept notes on the "community garden" her Green Thumb Club created.

Once Vern came in with a set of instructions on how to make a seed starter pot out of a page from a magazine and one of his grandson's alphabet blocks. They were just the right size mini-pots for tomato seeds. There are a number of ways that this can be done. One is an origami engineering project. It required a high degree of coordination and determination. You can Google *"pots from newspaper"* and find more variations on this theme than you can handle.

Colleen rescued some large cans from the kitchen and had everyone paint them. Then her Green Thumb Club clipped pictures from last year's seed catalogs. These were glued on the painted cans to make large planters that were lined up along the walkway for everyone to enjoy. She called it their "Tin Can Garden."

These are just a few ideas from Green Thumb Club members from everywhere. Set your creative mind free and see what happens.

Nutty as a Fruit Cake, an Opinion Poll

What would the holidays be without the Fruitcake? We give them as gifts, make jokes about them, sometimes we even eat them. This holiday tradition has a long history. When Joyce brought her two pound Christmas gift into the activity room to share, she was met with variety of reactions. Some were eager to have a sample. Some refused in no uncertain terms. One lady said she was allergic to fruitcake and another said she would love to have a piece, but it was forbidden by her diet.

Let's take a little Fruitcake Poll. Perhaps someone in the group has received one of these seasonal delights and is willing to share while answering and discussing these questions. You can choose one participant to keep score. Don't hesitate to discuss, debate or even argue about these questions.

1. How well do you like fruitcake?
a) Love it. Could eat the whole thing myself.
b) Like fruitcake in small doses
c) Will only eat it to be sociable
d) Hate it. It's not really edible, is it?
e) Isn't fruitcake a joke?

2. Have you ever made a fruitcake?
a) YES, it's a family tradition
b) I haven't but a family member did once
c) NO

3. What do you think is the most important ingredient in a good fruitcake?
a) The fruit
b) Brandy
c) The exotic spices
d) Molasses
e) Other _____

4. Have you ever given fruitcakes as gifts?
a) Yes
b) No
c) I refuse to answer on the grounds that it may incriminate me.

5. What do you do with a fruitcake you receive as a gift?
a) Eat it, of course
b) Give it to Mikey. He'll eat anything
c) Give it to a friend next Christmas
d) It burns nicely in the fireplace
e) Other _____

Let's talk about it

During an intergenerational school Grandma's Kitchen project the following became subjects of intense discussion and lighthearted exchanges.

If you were going to build a better fruitcake what would you do differently?

What happens if you add chocolate chips?

How do fruitcakes differ around the world?

The Fruitcake Quiz

For those who want to be intellectually challenged, we humbly offer the official fruitcake quiz. Warning: This is not easy. We suggest that this be taken as an open book test. Getting a little help from your friends is not cheating, it's a nice thing to do. Let's see how well you do with this little fruitcake quiz.

1. The first historical mention of fruit cake is in:
a) Ancient Egypt
b) 1st century India
c) 16th century England
d) Colonial America

2. The American Fruitcake Capital is:
a) Boston, MA
b) Claxton, GA
c) Williamsburg, VA
d) San Francisco, CA

3. Which of the following is not usually an ingredient in American fruitcakes
a) Candied fruit
b) Pecans
c) Applesauce
d) Molasses

4. A good fruitcake, if stored properly, can remain edible for:
a) 6 weeks
b) 6 months
c) Next Christmas
d) 25 years or more if frozen

5. An American humorist compiled a list of uses for a fruitcake that included all of the following except a:
a) Doorstop
b) Fireplace log
c) Sand bags in flood prone areas
d) Dessert
e) Home plate on little league baseball fields

6. 1969 was an historic year for the American fruitcake because
a) it was eaten in outer space by the crew of Apollo 11
b) the largest fruitcake ever was baked in Philadelphia
c) for the first time in history fruitcakes became a part of the USDA emergency food relief program
d) Disney produced the first fruitcake shaped like Micky Mouse

7. A high quality fruit cake should be at least what percentage by volume of fruits and nuts?
a) 25%
b) 50%
c) 80%
d) 110%

8. The average fruit cake produced in America weighs
a) 1 lb
b) 2 lb
c) 4 lb 2 oz
d) 5 lb

9. Manitou Springs, Colorado is famous for its annual
a) Fruitcake eating contest
b) Building a house out of last year's fruitcakes
c) Fruitcake decorating festival
d) Fruitcake toss

10. Fruitcake is often associated with certain monasteries around the world because
a) They make the brandy used in fruitcake construction.
b) The European monasteries where traditionally used as storage sites for a village's fruitcakes.
c) Fruitcake is mentioned so many times in the Bible that it is considered a holy food.
d). Many monasteries produce fruitcakes as a major source of funding for their work.

Check out the Society for the Protection and Preservation of Fruitcake on the web
http://www.fruitcakesociety.org

Answers:
1-a) it was used as food for the departed. 2-b) Claxton, GA (other also make this claim) 3-c). 4 all are correct. 5-d) Dessert. 6-a) These astronauts enjoyed the first fruitcake in outer space. 7-b) at least 50%. 8-b) 2 pounds. 9-d) the January Fruitcake Toss. 10-d) They use the fruit cakes as a fundraiser.

A fruitcake came My Way

A fruitcake came one day
And I sent it on its way.
The next day, then,
It was back again,
But here it cannot stay.

I sent it to one brother,
Who sent it to another.
It eventually
Came back to me,
In a package from my mother.

I sent it to a friend --
At least, he was 'til then.
He sent it back
With a caustic crack
And we never spoke again.

I sent it to my boss
And signed it "Santa Claus."
My name he guessed
And readdressed
That spice-baked albatross.

I sent it to a client,
Who proved to be defiant:
It seems the space
In his office place
Is fruitcake noncompliant.

I picked someone at random
In hopes that he could stand 'em.
It was returned:
Somehow he'd learned
I was the Fruitcake Phantom.

If a fruitcake comes today,
I think I'll let it stay.
It's crystal clear
Its place is here --
And I must move away.
By Paris Saizan

Eat Your Veggies!

A find a word with fruits and vegetables you might find on the dinner table

```
H M P M M N G D M E K N X T D
S I S A U E R K R A U T P E M
P O N I O N S Q U A S H I S I
I P A E S E O T A T O P M U N
N A E C U A S E L P P A G G T
R R B R O C C O L I Y R F A H
U S N A E B Y E N D I K J R K
T N E S S C O L E S L A W A A
A I E B E E P I C K L E S P L
B P R K O N D C A R R O T S E
A S G S T N I J E G A B B A C
G P P W A T E R M E L O N M H
A F E C M E E G S G L O G I A
S S C U O E P F E I R F J L R
K X S S T E E B E X I D R E D
```

Find the following hidden words:

applesauce	chard	mint	rutabagas
asparagus	coleslaw	onions	sauerkraut
beets	green beans	parsnips	squash
broccoli	kale	peas	tomatoes
cabbage	kidney beans	pickles	turnips
candied yams	limas	potatoes	watermelon
carrots			

Mashed Potatoes

The potato is the most popular vegetable in America, and is the fourth most popular food in the world after wheat, rice and corn. Let's see how well you know this versatile vegetable.

1. Potatoes are sometimes called SPUDS
a) in honor of the famous people's interviewer, Spuds Terkel.
b) from a South America Indian word that means "tastes good."
c) a play on a medical term for "sleeping with your eyes open."
d) an Irish term for a type of shovel used to dig potatoes

2. When was Mr. Potato Head born?
a) 1929,   b) 1888,   c) 1952,   d) 2020

3. The potato is related to
a) the sweet potato,   b) onions,   c) turnips,   d) tomatoes

4. Potatoes originated in
a) South America,   b) Spain,   c) Ireland,   d) Africa

5. Potatoes have been used to cure a number of illnesses, diseases and conditions. Such as
a) warts,   b) headache,   c) rheumatism   d) toothache

6. The potato was poorly received when introduced to France because it was thought to cause
a) Leprosy,   b) Sterility,   c) blindness,   d) lefthandedness

7. The average American eats approximately
a) 1 lb of potatoes a week,   b) 1 potato a day,   c) 1 ton a year,
d) 1 baked potato a week

8. French fries were first served at the White House by
a) Benjamin Franklin,   b) Teddy Roosevelt,   c) George W. Bush,
d) Thomas Jefferson

9. The Potato Capital of South Dakota is the town of Clark. This town is home to
a) the International Potato Museum
b) the largest potato ever grown
c) the world famous Mashed Potato Wrestling Contest
d) the Russet Family Potato Farm

10. Someone who spends all his or her time sitting and watching the TV is commonly called
a) a cold potato,   b) a couch potato,   c) a fat potato,   d) a potato brain

11. Potatoes produce lavender-blue star shaped flowers. These blossoms became a fashion statement when who wore them in her hair?
a) Queen Elizabeth II,   b) Jackie Kennedy,   c) Mary Todd Lincoln,
d) Marie Antoinette

12. Which vice president misspelled p-o-t-a-t-o-e?
a) Al Gore,   b) Dick Cheney,   c) Dan Quayle,   d) Spiro Agnew

Can you separate potato fact from potato fiction?

1. FACT or FICTION   Potatoes were so valued for their vitamin C content that miners traded gold for potatoes during the Klondike gold rush in1897-98.

2. FACT or FICTION   Potato chips were invented by accident.

3. FACT or FICTION   Potato leaves are poisonous.

4. FACT or FICTION   At first, the Europeans were reluctant to accept the potato because it wasn't mentioned in the Bible.

5. FACT or FICTION   The name for this popular vegetable comes from a Latin word meaning "knobby roots."

Bonus question:
What do Tom Brokaw, Walter Cronkite, Chet Huntley and David Brinkley have in common?

Digging a little deeper:

One of the Green Thumb Clubs in a senior community was left on their own one afternoon when the activity director was caught in traffic. They were meeting in the room beside the kitchen and in a matter of minutes their creative minds were on a rampage. It all started when a bag of potatoes was spotted sitting in the doorway. Soon potatoes were spread across the table. Conversation was spontaneous and contagious. First they compiled a list of ways to eat potatoes and took an vote to see which was the most popular. This is a fun project for any group to do.

Maria Lucero changed the discussion when she began telling a story about how her grandmother would place slices of potato on her forehead if she had a headache or a fever. "This would work most of the time," she explained. Soon others were sharing their potato stories, like the way Colleen's Irish uncle would remove warts with a potato. And there were many others. Perhaps you know of some "medicinal uses" for potatoes.

Next one of the club members left the room and returned minutes later with a handful of table knives and spoons. She showed them a project they had done when she was a student in a little one room school in Orange, Ohio. They then set to work cutting their potatoes in half. Then, on the clean flat surface they began to carve images of flowers, shapes or geometric patterns. Then they "borrowed" some paint and dipped their "potato stampers" in the paint then onto some plain white muslin that had been reserved for a craft project. For some it was a mess, for others it was art, but for everyone, it was fun.

Just a couple thoughts:

Do you remember the elementary school science experiment where you made a "potato battery" to power a small clock or radio? How did that work anyway?

Have you ever made a 'Patriotic Potato Salad? It's both fun and easy. You start with red skin potatoes, white potatoes and blue potatoes. You can add any other vegetables you wish and celebrate any holiday with this colorful dish.

Have you ever grown or eaten blue potatoes? Try it.

Answers:
1-d, 2-c, 3-d, 4-a, 5-a,b,c,d, 6-a, 7-b, 8-d, 9-c, 10-b, 11-d, 12-c,
1. Fact, 2. Fact, 3. Fact, 4. Fact, 5. Fiction

Bonus question: They are all common taters, of course.

A Literary Quiz for Gardeners of All Ages
This is a great conversation starter for an intergenerational program

1. Peter Rabbit was guilty of trespassing and theft when he stole _____ from Mr. MacGregor's garden.

2. Bre'r Rabbit escaped from Bre'r Fox when he said, "Please, Whatever you do, don't throw me in that there _____."

3. In the Dr. Seuss story "The Lorax" the Lorax is trying to save what unusual species of tree? _____

4. What did Jack (in the Jack & The Beanstalk story) trade for handful a beans? _____

5. Charlie Brown's friend Linus waited for who on Halloween? _____

6. Little Jack Horner sat in a corner eating his Christmas pie.
   He stuck in his thumb and pulled out a _____,
   And said, "What a good boy am I."

7. Thumbelina went sailing in a _____

8. "Run, run, as fast as you can.
   You can't catch me,
   I'm the _____ _____."

9. In Alice in Wonderland the Walrus told a tale of _____ and kings.

10. In the Disney version of the popular fairy tale, Cinderella rode to the ball in a coach the fairy godmother made from a _____

Answers:
1. Carrots,   2. Briar patch,   3. Truffala trees,   4. The family cow,   5. The Great Pumpkin,   6. Plum,
7. Pea shell,   8. Gingerbread Man,   9. Cabbages,   10. Pumpkin

Sherlock Humus and the case of the
Mysterious Blooming House Plant

a Sherlock Humus, plant detective, mystery

This can be done individually or as a group. If you are doing it as a group, each 'assistant detective' can record the number of the clues needed to solve the mystery.

Sherlock Humus, the world famous plant detective, had just enjoyed a fine dinner at his friend, Dr. Gardener Watson's London Estate when the call came in. In fact he had just put two after dinner mints in his mouth when the butler handed him the phone.

There was a pause, then he responded, "Yes. Most interesting. We will be right over." He handed the phone back to the butler and called to his friend who was tending the fire in the fireplace. "Get your coat, Watson. There is a mystery afoot. Lady Grandiflora needs our assistance."

They arrived at the brownstone and were led to the cramped and musty conservatory where Lord Grandiflora had housed and cared for his rare plant collection before his demise some months ago.

"There," she said pointing to a lonely little plant sitting at the edge of the potting bench. "I hadn't noticed it at all until this afternoon when I stepped out here to attend to the watering of this accursed menagerie of disgusting plants." She stepped forward and touch the leaf, "but this one is different. I like it and need to know what it is and how to care for it. I knew that of all the horticulturalists in England, you were the most knowledgeable and could tell me what this is."

Sherlock Humus took his magnifying glass from his coat pocket and began searching for clues. But, he needs your help. Let's see how quickly you can identify this mysterious plant. Here are the clues he found.

1. The wooden tag, though covered with dirt and mold, presented one decipherable word, *Tanganyika.* "We now know this African country as Tanzania." Sherlock Humus stated in his most professorial voice.

2. The roundish leaves were covered with hair. "See this," Sherlock Humus said as he touched the leaf. "It must be related to the Gloxinia."

3. "Look over here," Dr. Watson pointed to an egg carton with the same fuzzy roundish leaves stuck in the soil each cell contained. "I think it can be started from a leaf." He pointed to the minute little leaves forming around the one that had been stuck into the soil.

4. Lady Grandiflora smiled as she caressed the dark blue-purple blossoms. "I hadn't noticed flowers on it until today. But, aren't they beautiful, almost like a . . . ." But Sherlock Humus interrupted her. "Oh No! It's definitely not what you are thinking."

5. " Over here, in your late husband's diary is a notation, *This insignificant little plant named for the German governor Baron Walter von Saint Paul seemed hardly worthy of our cultivation. Some have decided to discard theirs but I cannot bring myself to destroy the parent and the children I have started.*"

6. Watson lifted the pot to get a better view of this little plant with its purple flowers. On the back of the pot was a penciled notation, "Discovered in East Africa 1892."

7. "Watson, you've broken the pot." Sherlock Humus almost shouted as he spied the bottom of the pot sitting on the bench. But upon examining closer he could see that it was actually one pot sitting inside another. "Perhaps a clever watering system," Watson suggested.

8. Further on in the diary was another note about *Saintpaulia*. Sherlock read aloud, *"I wish that it bloomed with brighter and varied colours. Perhaps some day we can persuade it to flower in pink, sky blue and white.* His wish, I'm certain, will come true." Humus took the plant from Dr. Watson's hand, "I'm becoming rather fond of this little charmer myself."

9. Lady Grandiflora held out her hand. "I wonder if I could rescue it from this dank and damp greenhouse and place it on my windowsill to brighten my winter days?" Sherlock Humus answered, as he peered at the deep purple flowers with their bright yellow stamens, "I suspect that a northern or eastern window would be ideal for it.

10. "Are you certain that this is not a violet?" Watson asked as they left the greenhouse with Lady Grandiflora carefully carrying it with her.

"I know what it is," Sherlock Humus exclaimed. "I have solved your mystery. It is most definitely an ...."

Note: answer on page 122

18

Famous Garden Quotes

"Gardening is the purest of human pleasures." -- Francis Bacon

A lot of prominent people, both famous and infamous, have made memorable comments about gardens and gardeners. Each of us not only have our own favorite garden quotes from others, but we all continue to harvest thoughts, impressions and comments of our own about this basic human art form.

Now let's see how well you do with these quotes. But identifying the creators of these lines is only the beginning. Perhaps you can recall the comments or writings of others about the same subject. Better yet, perhaps you can propagate a few memorable quotes of your own. Share your memories, your thoughts and your impressions with others. Perhaps even create a Garden Journal with collected lines from your garden of friends.

1. "We can complain because rose bushes have thorns, or rejoice because thorn bushes have roses." is usually attributed to
a) Gypsy Rose Lee,   b) Abraham Lincoln,   c) Jackson Perkins,   d) Queen Victoria

2. "I perhaps owe having become a painter to flowers."
a) Claude Monet,   b) Leonardo DiVinci,   c) Grant Wood,   d) Rembrandt

3. Thomas Cooper wrote "A garden is never so good as it will be _____."
a) after the rain,   b) in the morning sun,   c) viewed with a glass of iced tea
d) next year.

4. "Earth laughs in flowers." was written by a poet who spoke the language of flowers quite well. This poet was:
a) Carl Sandburg,   b) William Shakespeare   c) Ralph Waldo Emerson,   d) Edgar Guest

5. Thomas Jefferson wrote in his journal, "Though an old man, I am but a young _____."
a) lover,   b) statesman,   c) gardener,   d) architect

6. "Bread feeds the body, indeed, but flowers feed the soul" is a line that appears in
a) Bible,   b) teachings of Buddha,   c) Koran,   d) Sayings of Confucius

7. John Erskine wrote, "I have never had so many _____ _____ day after day as when I worked in the Garden."
a) aching joints,   b) pleasant experiences,   c) muddy clothes,   d) good ideas

8. "All through the long winter I dream of my garden. On the first day of spring, I dig my fingers deep into the soft earth. I can feel its energy, and my spirit soars." This quote if from which famous movie star?
a) Henry Fonda,   b) Helen Hayes,   c) Marilyn Monroe,   d) Meryl Streep

9. "To forget how to dig the earth and to tend the soil is to forget ourselves." These wise words were uttered by:
a) John Lennon,   b) W. Atlee Burpee,   c) Mohandas K. Gandhi,   d) Mother Theresa

10. Luther Burbank said "A flower is only _____ weed."
a) an educated,   b) a civilized,   c) good looking,   d) clever

"Life is the fruit of your own creation." John Denver

Answers: 1-b,   2-a,   3-d,   4-c,   5-c,   6-c.   7-d,   8.-b,   9-c,   10-a

Spice is the Variety of Life

A just for fun Fact or Fiction quiz on the great spices of the world

1. FACT or FICTION — There is no ginger in ginger ale.

2. FACT or FICTION — Nutmeg is the seed of an edible tropical fruit.

3. FACT or FICTION — Allspice is a blend of cloves, nutmeg, cinnamon and ginger.

4. FACT or FICTION — Cloves are the dried flower buds of a tropical shrub.

5. FACT or FICTION — Vanilla is made from the seed pods of a tropical tree.

6. FACT or FICTION — Capers are the flower buds of a Mediterranean shrub.

7. FACT or FICTION — Bay Rum is a men's cologne made from bay leaves.

8. FACT or FICTION — Cinnamon is made from the bark of a tree.

9. FACT or FICTION — Paprika is made from the powdered roots of a tree native to Hungary.

10. FACT or FICTION — Saffron is considered one of the world's most costly spices.

11. FACT or FICTION — Cream of Tartar is what's left when grape juice becomes wine.

12. FACT or FICTION — Hops, the flavoring for beer, is in the same plant family as Marijuana.

13. FACT or FICTION — Black pepper and white pepper come from the same plant.

14. FACT or FICTION — Sassafras tea is made from the roots of a native American tree.

15. FACT or FICTION — Licorice is the most popular Jelly Bean Flavor.

Answers:
1. Fiction, but now very little,   2. Fiction,   3. Fiction,   4. Fact,   5. Fiction,   6. Fact,   7. Fiction,
8. Fact,   9. Fiction,   10. Fact,   11. Fact,   12. Fact,   13. Fact,   14. Fact,   15. Fact

Some Spicy Thoughts

No matter where in the world we grew up, the spices were an important part of the meal. The following is a little opinion poll to see what spices are most popular with your group or family. We have had residents of various senior communities compare notes, but one of the most interesting was an intergenerational program with a middle school and a senior center. They had samples of various foods, drinks and desserts using assorted spices. The seniors had the children guess what spice was used in each of the samplings. They decided that the kids had a lot to learn.

1. Have you ever had sassafras tea? Did you like it? Would you like to try sassafras cookies?

2. Which flavor ice cream do you prefer, Vanilla or Chocolate?

3. What ways do you like to taste ginger? Have you even baked gingerbread man cookies from scratch? Or built a gingerbread house?

4. What spices would you use in making an apple pie?

5. What is your favorite flavor of jelly beans?

6. Do you like chile peppers? What foods would you use these hot peppers on?

7. What spice do you think has the best fragrance?

8. What foods would you use allspice in?

9. What spices do you think might be in Root Beer, Coca-Cola? Which do you like best?

10. Do you like any of the spice teas? Which one is your favorite?

You can use your own questions, and the participants are free to plan a spicy dinner party, complete with samples, if they wish.

Sherlock Humus
and the Case of Death with a Smile

Dr. Watson was examining the crime scene with magnifying glass in hand. There was a crumpled napkin on the floor beside the desk. The deceased was slumped back in his chair with a curious smile on his face. His hand still held the fork that rested near an empty gold embossed dessert plate. Sherlock Humus, world famous botanical detective was examining the small ornate cup and saucer, now empty. It still contained a small amount of residue. Sherlock raised the cup to his delicate nose and sniffed it gently. You can examine the clues and perhaps solve this mystery.

1. The receipt in the deceased's pocket told them that he had recently returned from the neighborhood delicatessen where he had purchased a single carry out item that cost $5.87.

2. Dr. Watson read from the deceased's notes, showing that he had recently returned from Mexico where he had been studying the ancient Olmec culture and its foods.

3. "The name Godiva is on the side of this crumpled piece of wrapper," Sherlock Humus commented as he carefully spread the piece of paper flat on the cluttered desk of the famous archaeologist.

4. Watson carefully opened the other paper retrieved from the floor. "Curious, Humus. This one says Giardelli."

5. Dr. Watson found a photo of a small tree with orange colored pods hanging directly from the trunk and main branches.

6. "The word *Theobroma* appears throughout these notes," Sherlock Humus muttered, "Why, I think that means *food of the gods*." He gazed out the window for a few seconds then continued, "Curious. Most curious, Watson."

7. While Watson was studying this curious photo, Sherlock Humus was reading a medical report. "Hummmm," he said as he adjusted his bifocals to better read the fine print, "It says here that consumption of the fruit of this tree is good for one's health as it is rich in anti-oxidents and even makes one feel happier." There was a pause as he read further. "Watson, it is further regarded as an aphrodisiac of sorts."

8. "It is one of the most popular Valentine's Day gifts for the object of one's affection, I have observed." Watson replied with a smile.

9. Sherlock Humus turned his attention again to the gilded dessert plate. He studied the dark brown crumbs that remained. Then he wiped his index finger across the frosting and crumbs and put it to his lips. A broad smile formed as he exclaimed, "I know what killed this unfortunate scientist. It was the famous dessert from the deli."

10. Watson opened the small drawer in the center of the desk and gasped. "Humus, look here. Our scientist was obviously an addict." The open drawer contained dozens of flat items, each with a dark brown wrapper and silver letters that spelled out H-E-R-S-H-E-Y.

"Yes, Watson. He is the victim of an overdose brought on by that infamous cake, with those chips and that decadent frosting. He unfortunately topped this dangerous dessert off with ice cream with the same dangerous ingredient. Obviously a deadly combination. It's elementary, Watson. It's a case of Death by . . . . ".

Answer on page 122

Danger in the Garden

In no way do we want to discourage anyone from being a part of the people-plant connection. However, there are plants that can be a threat. Some plants have spines, and others can cause a rash. Some of our most common plants can be a serious threat if leaves or flowers are eaten, even though the fruit is a healthy food. There are common plants that can cause eye inflamation, and some that can cause an upset stomach in a healthy twenty year old but pose a serious threat to a more mature individual who may be on medications.

Let's take a look at some of the dangerous plants that might be lurking in the garden, or on the windowsill.

1. Horseradish is in the mustard family. It can make your eyes water, and your throat burn. Which of the following vegetables is related to the horseradish and can affect you the same way?
a) Shallots,   b) Jalapeno peppers,   c) Watercress,   d) Wasabi

2. Poison Ivy is a well known villain. Everyone has not so fond childhood memories of encounters. A popular snack is a member of the same family. Do you know which of these is a poison ivy cousin?
a) Cashews,   b) Chocolate,   c) Kiwi fruit,   d) Mother-in-Law's Tongue (Sansevieria)

3. One of these popular house plants can cause your throat to close if eaten. Do you know which one is the culprit?
a) English ivy,   b) Kangaroo vine,   c) Swedish ivy,   d) Philodendron

4. One of these windowsill flowering plants is NOT poisonous if eaten. Do you know which one?
a) Amaryllis,   b) African violet,   c) Azalea,   d) Angel's trumpet

5. All of the following flowers are edible except
a) Geraniums,   b) Cyclamen,   c) Fuschia,   d) Hibiscus

7. MYTH or REALITY   Any plant with milky sap is poisonous.

8. MYTH or REALITY   Tomato leaves are poisonous.

9. MYTH or REALITY   Chive flowers are toxic if eaten raw.

10. MYTH or REALITY   Poinsettias are deadly poisonous.

11. MYTH or REALITY   Sweet potato leaves are toxic.

12. MYTH or REALITY   Hens & Chicks sap can cause warts.

13. MYTH or REALITY   Some cactus plants can literally shoot their spines into you.

14. MYTH or REALITY   Chewing the leaves of Dumbcane (Diffenbachia) can make your mouth numb.

15. MYTH or REALITY   The fruit of ornamental peppers is poisonous.

Bonus question!
Do you remember the little verse about poison ivy, "Leaflets three, let it be?"
Does the same advice hold true for poison oak and poison sumac?

Answers:
1-d,   2-a,   3-d,   4-b,   5-b,   6. Myth,   7. Myth, lettuce and dandelions have a milky sap,
8. Reality,   9. Myth, they are both colorful and flavorful,   10. Myth, may be allergenic reactions but
they are not deadly,   11. Myth, in fact they are very nutritious,   12. Myth,   13. Myth, no cactus can
shoot their spines,   14. Reality,   15. They may be very hot, but not toxic.   Bonus question, Yes

Who's Blooming in Your Garden?

Every family has some really beautiful flowers. Every circle of friends also has some special people blooming there. True, most have a few weeds too, but we won't worry about them. Take a look at your own family or neighborhood garden and see if it has beautiful flowers that match these below.

1. The rose is an ideal blend of outer beauty and inner charm. The rose tells you that someone cares and it's ok to smile. Is there a member of your family, or a friend that reminds you of a rose?
Who deserves your Rose Award? _____

2. The dandelion is mistreated, scorned and unappreciated, yet it keeps on blooming. Is there a member of your family, or a friend, who has had rough times and survived, continuing to smile all the while?
Who deserves your Dandelion Smiling Award? _____

3. No vegetable garden is complete without a zucchini plant. These are the providers in the garden, giving a never-ending supply of fare to feed all who are hungry. Is there a friend, someone in your family, who could always be depended upon to provide the family dinner, fill the church table, or appear on the doorstep with a bag of produce, or a hot dish, for one who has suffered some misfortune?
Who Deserves your Zucchini Award? _____

4. The lilies of the field care nothing about tomorrow, but they are very good at accepting the gift of today. They put their faith in God and sunshine while they go about sharing smiles and spreading joy. Who among your family or friends is always there when needed, is the shoulder to cry on, or a sympathetic ear willing to listen and accept without passing judgement?
Who has earned your Smiling Lily Award? _____

5. The oak tree provides shade and shelter. We trust in its support when we need something to lean on. We all need an oak tree in our lives and most of us are fortunate enough to have such a family member, or trusted friend. Who can you depend on the most?
Who has earned your Oak Tree Award? _____

6. The sweet potato in the Mason jar of water sends its vines around the winter time windowsill. Even during the cold bleak days of winter, it gives us green, heart shaped leaves, a promise that spring will return. Do you have a family member who was always optimistic, even in the worst of times? Is there a friend who could always be counted on to find the silver lining, no matter how dark the cloud was?
Who should be given your Sweet Potato Vine Award? _____

Taking your garden a little farther:

- A great activity project could involve actually making award certificates or medals for deserving family members or friends. You can include photos, silk flowers, artwork. It's up to you. Use the computer, or scissors and paste.

- You can create other awards as well. Be creative, and be positive.

- If you are in a senior care facility, hospital or rehab center, why not create a set of awards for the staff and volunteers who work there? Staff are all too often overworked and under-appreciated.

- You can make it a project for the entire facility or school by setting up a fish bowl or jar for each award. Put a picture of the flower and brief description on all of the jars. Let each resident, staff member or student vote by writing on a slip of paper and casting their vote by placing it in the jar with the individual's name on it. A special awards day can be held to honor the winners and nominees.

- This is also a great springboard for discussion.

Let the conversation flower, the ideas blossom and the creativity bear fruit.

Share your beautiful garden of family and friends with us and we can pass on your ideas to enrich the lives of others. Email us a copy of your awards, a brief description of who the recipients are and why they have earned it.

What's in Your Fruit Basket, Apples or Pears?

This is a little quiz on varieties of fruit.
All you have to do is decide: *Is it an apple or a pear*

This is a great quiz to use with a tasting session with samples of assorted varieties of apples and pears, apple juice, cider and pear juice, apple pie, apple butter and any other taste treat made form these two popular fruits. An opinion poll and open discussion are welcome. Circle which you think this is APPLE or PEAR. Note: Some of these are heirloom varieties.

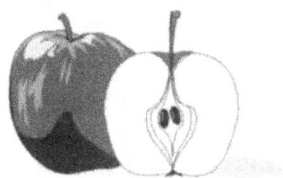

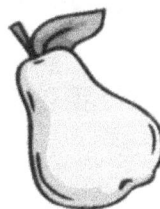

1. APPLE   PEAR   Moonglow

2. APPLE   PEAR   Golden Delicious

3. APPLE   PEAR   Catface

4. APPLE   PEAR   Kieffer

5. APPLE   PEAR   McIntosh

6. APPLE   PEAR   Bosc

7. APPLE   PEAR   Pippin

8. APPLE   PEAR   Orient

9. APPLE   PEAR   Winesap

10. APPLE   PEAR   Seckel

11. APPLE   PEAR   Nonesuch

12. APPLE   PEAR   Double Delicious

13. APPLE   PEAR   Northern Spy

14. APPLE   PEAR   D'Anjou

15. APPLE   PEAR   Ayers

16. APPLE   PEAR   Rome Beauty

17. APPLE   PEAR   Bartlett

18. APPLE   PEAR   Sheepnose

19. APPLE   PEAR   Gala

20. APPLE   PEAR   Comice

Open for discussion:

What is your favorite apple? Why?

What is your favorite pear? Why?

What's your favorite way to eat apples?

How do you like pears best?

Have you ever grown apples or pears?

Have you ever made apple butter or cider?

What would happen if you grafted an apple branch onto a pear tree?

What's in Your Fruit Basket? Apples or Pears
1. Apples, 2. Apple, 3. Apple, 4. Pear, 5. Apple, 6. Pear, 7. Apple, 8. Pear, 9. Apple,
10. Pear,   11. Apple, 12. Apple,   13. Apple,   14. Pear,   15. Pear,   16. Apple,   17. Pear,
18. Apple,   19. Apple,   20. Pear

Taste of the Tropics

Don't you enjoy something a little different? The taste of exotic fruits and vegetables can be a delight. Some of these can even be grown on your windowsill, at least when young. Someone in your group might be quite familiar with these tropical tastes. The great thing about these little quizzes is that we can learn from each other. Simply decide if these statements about tropical fruits and vegetables are TRUE or FALSE. Of course, this is open for discussion.

1. TRUE FALSE   Alligator Pear is another name for the avocado.

2. TRUE FALSE   Pineapples grow on huge trees.

3. TRUE FALSE   Kiwi fruit grows underground after the flowers are pollinated.

4. TRUE FALSE   Coconuts are the source of chocolate.

5. TRUE FALSE   Papayas grow on vines that may exceed 100 feet in length.

6. TRUE FALSE   Key lime is another name for Mexican lime.

7. TRUE FALSE   Ginger is made from the weird shaped fruit of this vine.

8. TRUE FALSE   Mangos are in the same family as Poison Ivy.

9. TRUE FALSE   The tasty starfruit grows on a sprawling vine.

10. TRUE FALSE   Dragon fruit grows on a vining cactus.

11. TRUE FALSE   Tapioca is a flour made from Cassava roots.

12. TRUE FALSE   Cashews grow on plants similar to tomatoes.

13. TRUE FALSE   Almonds grow underground, much like peanuts.

14. TRUE FALSE   Grapefruit grow in large clusters on sprawling vines.

15. TRUE FALSE   Jicama is the root of a tropical member of the bean family.

Answers:
1-T, 2-F, 3.-F, 4-F, 5-F, 6-T, 7-F, 8-T, 9-F, 10-T, 11-T, 12-F, 13-F, 14-F, 15-T

Tea Time

Enjoy a cup of your favorite tea with this find a word

```
D  W  Y  J  E  P  Z  R  C  C  W  I  F  M  N
O  A  X  F  U  O  E  V  Y  H  I  F  R  I  O
N  M  R  C  M  N  K  E  G  A  A  G  B  N  I
B  O  A  J  I  Y  R  E  G  M  C  I  K  T  S
X  E  T  A  E  B  E  R  P  O  C  M  T  L  U
T  P  R  P  A  E  R  T  M  D  A  B  B  F
F  T  T  M  I  E  L  K  G  I  N  X  L  S  N
S  T  A  I  N  L  A  I  L  L  E  M  A  C  I
T  T  E  X  S  T  O  I  N  E  R  R  C  G  G
E  T  E  A  P  A  R  T  Y  G  O  A  K  I  N
K  C  K  U  S  K  N  B  R  O  P  N  E  N  O
N  O  M  E  L  P  J  E  I  T  E  H  X  S  L
T  E  T  L  E  Y  O  B  W  M  E  G  Q  E  O
W  H  I  T  E  I  O  O  P  V  T  P  M  N  O
B  P  I  H  E  S  O  R  N  X  S  A  K  G  Y
```

Can you find the following hidden words?

BLACK	LEMON	STRAINER
CAMELLIA	LIPTON	TEACUP
CHAI	MINT	TEAPARTY
CHAMOMILE	OOLONG	TEASPOON
DARJEELING	PEKOE	TETLEY
EARLGREY	ROOIBOS	TISANE
GINSENG	ROSEHIP	WHITE
GREEN	STEEP	YERBAMATE
INFUSION		

Tea Trivia Quiz

The following is a little quiz to test your knowledge, experiences and memory. Sit back, pour a cup of tea and enjoy. May we humbly suggest that you invite some friends and make it a tea party?

1. FACT or FICTION   Coffee was popular in England before tea became the favored drink.

2. FACT or FICTION   Tea originated in Japan.

3. FACT or FICTION   The Boston Tea Party was only one of several such protests.

4. FACT or FICTION   The A & P grocery chain started out as single store called the Great American Tea Company.

5. FACT or FICTION   Iced Tea was an accidental invention during unseasonably cold weather in London.

6. FACT or FICTION   Yerba Mate tea is made from the leaves of a South American relative to the holly.

7. FACT or FICTION   Tea parties originated as a children's pastime.

8. FACT or FICTION   Teas are made from many different kinds of leaves

9. FACT or FICTION   Thomas Jefferson attempted to grow tea plants in the Southern States.

10. FACT or FICTION   Black tea contains more caffeine than green tea.

11. The tea bag was developed
a) in China centuries before it became popular in America.
b) in London as a way to sell more tea
c) in a Baltimore restaurant famous for its secret tea blend
d) by accident when a tea importer, Thomas Sullivan packaged his special blend in little silk sample bags.

12. Tea was supposedly discovered by

a) Chinese emperor, Shen Nung, in 2737 BC when leaves fell into a pot of water he was boiling.

b) British explorer James Cook in 1756.

c) A Japanese bonsai master when leaves from one of his bonsai plants fell into a cup of chrysanthemum blossom soup.

d) A Buddhist priest who was chewing tea leaves while meditating.

13. What country has the highest per capita tea consumption of these four?

a) England

b) United States of America

c) Ireland

d) Canada

14. Globally, tea is second to which of these in popularity?

a) Beer

b) Wine

c) Coffee

d) Water

15. What percentage of tea consumed in the United States is iced tea?

a) 25%

b) 52%

c) 80%

d) 96%

Conversations at the tea party

What is your favorite brand of tea? Why?

Do you prefer tea or coffee? Or some other drink?

Have you ever made any herbal teas? Which do you like best?

How many cups of tea (or glasses of iced tea, do you drink a week?

Answers:

1. Fact, 2. Fiction, 3. Fact, (there were similar protests in Philadelphia, New York, Maine, Maryland and North Carolina), 4. Fact (in 1859), 5. Fiction ,(it was invented by English merchant during a heat wave at the St Louis Worlds Fair in 1908), 6. Fact, 7. Fiction, 8. Fact, 9. Fact, 10. Fact, 11-d, 12-a, 13- c, 14-d, 15-c

Boston Baked Beans, Human Beans and Has Beans

The following little quiz is just for fun. We suggest that it be taken as a group. Please don't keep score. Just enjoy, laugh together and share your thoughts and comments. That's what friends are for. One last comment from us, "It has bean fun composing this little quiz. Sit back, relax and enjoy some jelly beans along the way."

1. A bean counter is
a) an employee in a jelly bean factory
b) a gardener who is overly serious about planting the rows of beans in her garden
c) a dietician who records the nutritional value of each serving of beans on the dinner plate
d) an accountant

2. Boston baked beans originated with
a) the Pilgrims who landed at Plymouth. It was a tradition brought from Europe.
b) John Adams during the Revolutionary War
c) the Iroquois, Penobscot and Narragansett Indians
d) the Kennedy family

3. The bean bag is
a) a chair
b) used to relieve the discomfort of arthritis
c) a game similar to horseshoes
d) a cloth bag designed to carry a large quantity of beans

4. Jelly Beans were
a) first found growing with carrots
b) first made in the Holy Land
c) began with the movie industry in the 1920's
d) were invented by the Easter Bunny

5. Which of these isn't a member of the bean family?
a) green beans
b) coffee beans
c) Lima beans
d) kidney beans

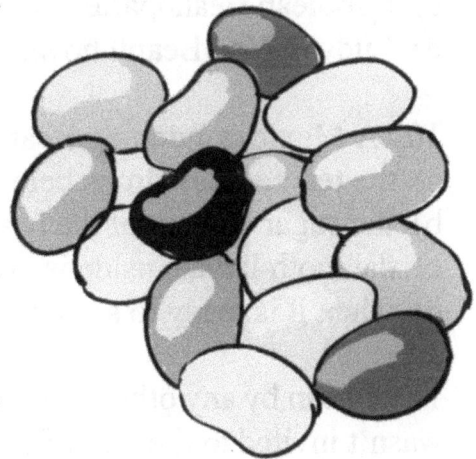

6. In the story Jack & the Bean Stalk what did Jack trade for the handful of beans?
a) the family cow
b) his mother's wedding ring
c) his grandmother's fine China
d) a portfolio of worthless stocks and bonds

7. The manufacture of Bush's Baked Beans has a closely guarded secret that who keeps trying to reveal?
a) the competitor, the HJ Heinz Company
b) Duke, the family dog
c) the son who was left out of the will
d) Col. Sanders

8. What is officially Baked Bean Month?
a) January
b) March
c) September
d) July

9. Who in this list was a real human being?
a) L. L. Bean
b) Jack Beany
c) Napolean Beanoparte
d) Ludwig Von Beanthhoven

10. A Mexican Jumping Bean jumps when
a) the temperature drops below 60 degrees, because it's shivering
b) the sugar content of the bean begins to ferment into alcohol
c) the moth larvae inside is awake
d) when it is ready to sprout

11. A bean by any other name is still member of the family. Which of the following wasn't invited to the Bean family reunion?
a) Sweet Pea
b) Lentil
c) Chickpea
d) Cashew

12. One of the all time favorite comic strips is Charles Schultz creation Peanuts. Peanuts are not really nuts, they are beans. That's how we can get away with this question in a bean quiz. One of the following comic stip characters is visiting from another strip. Which one of these isn't a Peanut?
a) Charlie Brown
b) Snoopy
c) Joey
d) Lucy

I've bean wondering:
1. Does anyone really like the ever-present green bean casserole?
2. Is it true? "You can lead a small child to green beans but you can't make him eat them."
3. Do you have a favorite bean recipe?
4. What kind of a bean do you grow if you plant a bean sprout?
5. What's your favorite Bean & Jerry Ice Cream flavor?
6. Have you ever made a bean bag?
7. What's your favorite un-bean? These are called beans but they aren't really related. Coffee beans, vanilla beans or chocolate beans?

If you were making a list of human beans who would you include? We'll get you started with
Leonard Beanstein and *Daniel Bean.* The rest is up to you. Working together try to create at least a dozen?

You can do this with song titles, movies, great books, even TV programs. Unleash your imagination and see what you come up with.

Answers:
1-d) A bean counter is an accountant, or someone fixated on numbers.
2-c) Boston baked beans were a tradition long before there was a Boston. The Native Americans made them with beans, maple syrup and bear grease.
3-a, b, c, d) Trick question. They are all bean bags
4-b) Jelly beans were first enjoyed in the Holy Land.
5-b) Coffee isn't in the bean family. It is really a gardenia
6-a) Jack traded the family cow for a handful of beans
7-b) the family dog, Duke, seems to have a problem with ethics. But the son is innocent.
8-d) July is official Baked Bean Month in the United States
9-a) Leon Leonwood Bean founded the LL Bean Company in 1912
10-c) The larvae of a moth is inside the Mexican jumping bean. With a little luck it will climb out of the bean as a moth.
11-d) The cashew isn't a bean, it's in the poison ivy family
12-c) Joey was the creation of Hank Ketchum and was the best friend in the Dennis the Menace comic strip.

Strolling Through the Spring Garden

The landscape is a reflection of the seasons, each with its own palate of colors, tapestry of textures, symphony of sounds, and delightful flavors and diverse textures. Spring is a special season because it is the awakening of winter's long rest. Life is refreshed and ready to LIVE.

In the following quiz we will stroll through spring and perhaps tickle a few of your memories. Please view these questions not as a test to be passed or failed, but as a journey both back in time and forward into tomorrow. Each day, regardless of where we are today, is the first day of spring for us, the first day in the rest of the journey down a garden path we've never walked before.

1. Parrots, Darwins, Lily Flowered, Cottage and Species are all classes of
a) Tulips,   b) Daffodils,   c) Hyacinths,   d) Crocus

2. King Alfred, Jonquil, Small cup and Poeticus are all types of
a) Tulips,   b) Daffodils,   c) Hyacinths,   d) Crocus

3. Amethyst, Carnegie, Delft Blue, Grape and Pink Pearl are all colors and kin of
a) Tulips,   b) Daffodils,   c) Hyacinths,   d) Crocus

4. Pickwick, Snow, Yellow Mammoth, Remembrance and Autumn are all varieties or cousins of the
a) Tulips,   b) Daffodils,   c) Hyacinths,   d) Crocus

5. Which of these was the subject of a "mania" of financial speculation in the 1630's with a single bulb selling for thousands of dollars?
a) Tulips,   b) Daffodils,   c) Hyacinths,   d) Crocus

6. Which of the following spring shrubs produces an edible fruit?
a) Flowering Almond,   b) Forsythia,   c) Azalea,   d) Nanking Bush cherry

7. Children could go barefoot when what flowers were in bloom?
a) The first roses of spring,   b) Tulips,   c) Dogwoods,   d) Lilacs

8. A traditional spring tonic was made from the roots of
a) Dogwood,   b) Horseradish,   c) Sassafras,   d) Forsythia

9. The worldwide symbol for Parkinson's Day, April 11 (the birthday of Dr. Parkinson) is the
a) White Dogwood, b) Yellow Daffodil, c) Red Tulip, d) Purple Lilac

10. Which of these was said to be the real contents of the Leprechaun's pot of gold?
a) Gold finches, b) Daffodils,   c) Forsythia,   d) Dandelions

11. Who returns to Capistrano on March 15th?
a) Doves,   b) Swallows,   c) Sparrows,   d) Robins

12. The tiny stamens of which of these flowers is the source of saffron?
a) Roses,   b) Apple blossoms,   c) Easter lilies,   d) Crocus

13. The Romans carried daffodil bulbs with them into battle to use
a) as an offering to Jupiter
b) a way to commit suicide if captured or wounded
c) as a snack if there was no food available
d) as a tribute to the enemy if captured

14. Which of these spring flowers is poisonous if eaten?
a) Azalea,   b) Violets,   c) Daisies,   d) Geraniums

15. Which of these spring flowers is not fragrant
a) Hyacinth,   b) Lilac,   c) Lily of the Valley,   d) Dogwood

16. FACT FICTION   Lady Pompadour made the hyacinth popular in
France when she started growing them in glass jars.

17. FACT FICTION   Hyacinths are the most fragrant of the spring flowering bulbs.

18. FACT FICTION   Lily of the Valley is said to signify a return to happiness.

19. FACT FICTION   Pussy willows are not related to the weeping willow.

20. FACT FICTION   Dandelion leaves are a healthy spring green for the dinner table.

Now it's your turn:

What are your favorite spring flowers?

What was the first flower to bloom where your spent your childhood?

What was your first sign of spring?

Did you ever go hiking in spring just to enjoy the wild flowers?

What was the first insect you usually encountered in springtime?

Did you ever use dandelions as toys? How?

Answers:

1-a, 2-b, 3-c, 4-d, 5-a, 6-d, 7-d, 8-c, 9-c, 10-d, 11-b, 12-d, 13-b, 14-a, 15-d, 16 Fact, 17 Fact, 18 Fact, 19 Fiction, 20 Fact

Sherlock Humus
and the Case of the April Fool's Day Flower

Dr. Watson was determined to play an April Fool's Day joke on his good friend Sherlock Humus, Plant Detective. Every year he tried, and every year Sherlock outsmarted the good doctor. This year it was going to be different. Watson arose early and strolled through the park, carefully selecting a few items. He then stopped by the tea shop, then to the green grocer's.

When he arrived at the famous plant detective's residence he had a collection of clues and a small black cardboard box.

The fragrance of fresh lilacs wafted through the air, mingling with morning tea and the sweet cakes that were a favorite of the great detective. Sherlock welcomed his friend with a smile and offered some fresh tea. This smile was not unlike the smile one would find on the cat who has just encountered a mouse.

1. "Humus, I have a special tea that I would like to share with you this morning." Watson was fumbling with the little, unmarked tea bags. "This tea is made from the roots of a special plant. The plant that will stump you this time, Humus."

2. As these two friends sipped the bitter tea, sweetened with a dash of honey, Watson pointed to the painting on the wall. It showed a lion snarling, showing its immense fangs. "Is that a new work of art?"

Humus laughed, "Yes, it is a gift from a client. Thankful for the return of a stolen box of rare African seeds."

3. "Humus, I encountered a less than rare bloom myself on the way here this morning. One that I believe was once said to keep witches and evil spirits at bay." Watson smiled again, "That, my good friend, is your third clue."

4. "Still, this is a common enough plant, this cousin of the daisies in your vase and the lettuce in your salad."

"Watson, this leaves thousands of relatives in a very large plant family, both wild and domestic, weed and table fare." Humus was now frowning. He had never gone to the fifth clue before identifying the mystery plant Dr. Watson concealed in his now infamous black box. "Do you have another clue for me?"

5. "It is the belief among the common folk and the herbalists that the sap from this little beauty is most effective in eliminating warts, and even freckles."

Humus frowned again. "I fear that you still have me stumped. Does this plant have other medicinal values?"

6. "Ah yes. It is known as a diuretic. So much so that the country folk refer to it as piss-a-bed."

7. Humus now smiled broadly and scribbled something on a notepad. "Watson, does the flower become a dark brown farmer's wine?"

8. "Would the earliest spring leaves of this most common of our flowers be cherished as a healthy green, to be savored with diced turnips and leeks?"

9. The housekeeper, Mrs. Hudson, entered the room with the morning mail and a knowing smile. "Dr Watson, would the plant in your black box be the favorite toy of children everywhere? Both flowers and seedheads being a plaything of youth?"

10. Watson was flustered now, but continued, "Strolling through the park this morning I was reminded of a comment made by James Russell Lowell,
> *Dear common flower, that grow'st beside the way,*
> *Fringing the dusty road with harmless gold,*
> *First pledge of blithesome May.*

"Watson, you almost had me. It wasn't until the seventh clue that I had it for certain. Open your black box so we can all enjoy the golden sunshine of these cheerful flowers. Perhaps Mrs. Hudson will prepare the package of greens you procured from the grocer this morning. Perhaps she will join us in a healthy repast and share a cup of this . . . . tea."

In case you haven't solved this mystery, the answer is on page 122

Creating the Perfect Salad

Sometimes the gardener grows the plants, and on occasion will pause to smell the flowers. But it's also necessary to harvest, prepare the meal and dine. When we can dine with friends it's a special joy.

Some think our salad days are behind us when we are no longer referred to as "Young Fella." Truth is, we are never too old for a good salad. Not only is this part of a healthy diet, a good salad can be a real dining delight. It can also be an artistic creation. As Bradley, one of our Green Thumb Club members said, "Building a great salad is like building a house, ya have to make a lot of decisions." Joyce wanted to make it perfectly clear, "There's a lot more to a good salad than a head of Iceberg Lettuce and bottle of Ranch Dressing. I've been trying to tell that to our cook for over a year now."

We all have our own preferences in salad fixin's. Here's your opportunity to take a poll of salad ingredients among your group. Vote on your favorites in each group and tabulate these votes. The results can then be compared to your dinner fare and perhaps your favorite chef can work these choices into a special salad just for your "Green Thumb Club."

Some like their salad spicy, some do not,
Others want it bland, or simple, or tangy, or hot.
There are those who prefer slightly bitter fare,
And others who seek vegetables exotic and rare.

Some want only crisp, green Iceberg lettuce to be seen,
But you might enjoy pasta, potato, spinach or bean.
Perhaps on the salad plate it's apples, raisins, walnuts and fruits,
Maybe for your palate it's carrots, radishes, or other tasty roots.

Choose from the list below, remember, anything goes,
Take this opportunity, your perfect salad to compose.

You are encouraged to express creativity by writing your own salad days poetry. Perhaps you would rather sketch or paint a work of art. Maybe you would like to play with your food and design a truly unique, perhaps whimsical three dimensional work of art in your salad bowl. If you would like to share them with us we would be delighted to see just how creative you can be when you "play with your food." You can email us your poetry, art or photos.

This is not a test, this is your SALAD BALLOT

1. The basic salad green
- ☐ Iceberg lettuce
- ☐ Leaf lettuce
- ☐ Romaine lettuce
- ☐ Cabbage
- ☐ Spinach
- ☐ No greens
- ☐ Other _____

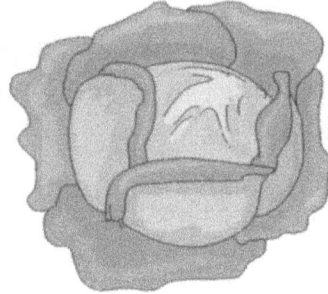

2. Other greens for flavor and texture
- ☐ Amaranth
- ☐ Arugula (Rocket)
- ☐ Bok Choy (Chinese Cabbage)
- ☐ Chard
- ☐ Chicory
- ☐ Cilantro
- ☐ Dandelion
- ☐ Endive
- ☐ Escarole
- ☐ Kale
- ☐ Mustard
- ☐ Watercress
- ☐ Other _____

3. Roots & tubers
- ☐ Beets
- ☐ Carrots
- ☐ Jicama
- ☐ Parsnips
- ☐ Potatoes
- ☐ Radishes
- ☐ Sweet potatoes
- ☐ Water Chestnuts
- ☐ Wasabi
- ☐ Other _____

4. Other veggies
- ☐ Artichokes
- ☐ Asparagus
- ☐ Bell peppers
- ☐ Broccoli
- ☐ Cauliflower
- ☐ Celery
- ☐ Chick peas (Garbanzo beans)
- ☐ Chile peppers
- ☐ Cucumbers
- ☐ Edaname
- ☐ Green beans
- ☐ Jalapeno peppers
- ☐ Kidney beans
- ☐ Mushrooms
- ☐ Okra
- ☐ Onions
- ☐ Peas
- ☐ Squash
- ☐ Tomatoes
- ☐ Tomatillo
- ☐ Zucchini
- ☐ Other _____

5. Fruits & nuts

- ☐ Apples
- ☐ Blueberries
- ☐ Cantalope
- ☐ Cashews
- ☐ Cranberries
- ☐ Figs
- ☐ Grapes
- ☐ Oranges
- ☐ Peaches
- ☐ Pears
- ☐ Pecans
- ☐ Pineapple
- ☐ Pistachios
- ☐ Raisins
- ☐ Raspberries
- ☐ Strawberries
- ☐ Watermelon
- ☐ Other _____

Meats for my salad

- ☐ Chicken
- ☐ Beef
- ☐ Ham
- ☐ Bacon
- ☐ Turkey
- ☐ Tuna
- ☐ Shrimp
- ☐ Prefer vegetarian salads
- ☐ Other _____

5. Dressings

- ☐ Blue Cheese
- ☐ Lemon Juice
- ☐ Mayonnaise, salad dressing
- ☐ Olive oil
- ☐ Ranch dressing
- ☐ Sour cream
- ☐ Vinegar
- ☐ Other _____

Herbs, spices and toppings

- ☐ Chives
- ☐ Croutons
- ☐ Fennel
- ☐ Flowers, geranium, violets, nasturtiums, etc.
- ☐ Ginger
- ☐ Sesame seed
- ☐ Thyme
- ☐ cheese
- ☐ boiled eggs
- ☐ Other _____

Specialty salads I like

- ☐ Potato salad
- ☐ Seafood Salad
- ☐ Pasta salad
- ☐ Taco salad
- ☐ Jello salad
- ☐ Bean salad
- ☐ Greek salad
- ☐ Fruit salad
- ☐ Other salad _____

What's important in your salad?

- ☐ Flavor
- ☐ Healthy diet
- ☐ Color
- ☐ Overall appearance
- ☐ Fun of preparing my own
- ☐ Sharing with a friend or several friends
- ☐ Don't like salads
- ☐ Other _____

UnFavorites: Salad stuff I don't like

1. My least favorite salad green is _____

2. My least favorite salad root vegetable is _____

3. My least favorite salad vegetable is _____

4. My least favorite salad dressing is _____

5. My least favorite kind of salad is _____

Think about it questions:

6. My favorite kind of salad is _____

7. If I were trimming a salad I would top it with _____

8. If I were going to make a boring salad exciting, I would add

_____

9. The best restaurant salad I ever had was a_____ at

_____

10. If I could share a salad with anyone in the whole world I would share it with

_____

The Lighter Side of Gardening

This little garden game was suggested by one of our Green Thumb Club friends. Her firm belief is that we take the garden, and life, far too seriously. She says, "We need to lighten up, smile at our flowers. They are a lot like us." Perhaps you can help us out here and provide some good suggestions. This can be even more fun when you do it as a committee. Keep in mind, there is probably more than one right answer.

1. If I want to hear some juicy gossip I might want to talk with the _____ One suggestion was watermelon, but what do you think?

2. What herb might I want to consult for a little wisdom _____

3. What common weed might you think of if your were looking for a parachute? _____.

4. What vegetable could you say has eyes in the back of its head? _____

5. You need to be careful what you say in the _____ field. Why?

6. What vegetable is always trying to get ahead? _____

7. You can tell what time it is when this flower is blooming. _____

8. What flower might be considered a 'Night Owl?' _____.

9. This western weed can probably outrun you. _____.

10. Following the sun is nothing new to this great American flower. _____.

Bonus. What do you get if you cross a four leaf clover with poison ivy?

_____

Popular answers, but you might think of something better. 1. Grapes, 2. Sage, 3. Dandelion, 4. Potatoes, 5. Corn, 6. Cabbage, 7. Four O'clocks, 8. Moon Flower, 9. Tumbleweed, 10. Sunflower. Bonus question: A rash of good luck.

All in the Family

Most of the fun lovin' flowers we have on our windowsills or in the flower beds have hard working kin in the vegetable garden or the orchard. Let's see if you can match the workers and the playboys in the two lists below.

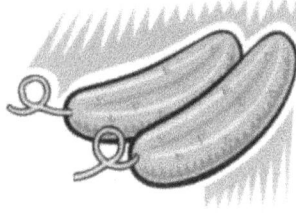

1. Cabbage

2. Green beans

3. Blackberries

4. Wheat

5. Cucumber

6. Sunflower

7. Sweet potatoes

8. Onions

9. Tomato

10. Blueberry

A. Roses

B. Sweet Peas

C. Petunias

D. Marigold

E. Azalea

F. Allium

G. Stocks

H. Pampas Grass

I. Gourds

J. Morning Glories

Answers: 1-G, 2-B, 3-A, 4-H, 5-I, 6-D, 7-J, 8-F, 9-C, 10-E

What's Growing in My Flower Garden?

A multitude of flowering plants have found their way into our gardens and onto our patios. Every part of the world has delightful flowers to share. In this vegetable soup game you can follow the alphabet and write down an outdoor flowering plant that begins with each letter of the alphabet. You can do this individually, as teams, with a time limit or any other way you choose. Enjoy the game, and afterwards, enjoy sharing your favorite flowers. We gave you A and Z, the rest is up to you. You can jot down more than one for each letter if you wish.

Alyssum _____
B _____
C _____
D _____
E _____
F _____
G _____
H _____
I _____
J _____
K _____
L _____
M _____
N _____
O _____
P _____
Q _____
R _____
S _____
T _____
U _____
V _____
W _____
X _____
Y _____
Zinnia _____

Dirty Words Gardeners Use

```
D S A W T E H L M L Q E
R M Y E M S I T E U T N
A R A I R O O A L A D O
I O L R S A C P G I H I
N W C P A H T E M U T S
A H O Y I B R I M O M O
G T A N R G L U O X C R
E R G Q G J S E E N V E
T A X A N E G O R T I N
A E P O T A S S I U M X
E L B A I R F H C L U M
P Z M F E R T I L E W N
```

AERATION	LEACHING
AGGREGATE	LIME
ARABLE	MUD
CLAY	MULCH
COMPOST	NITROGEN
DRAINAGE	PEAT
EARTHWORMS	POTASSIUM
EROSION	SOIL
FERTILE	TILTH
FRIABLE	TOPSOIL
HUMUS	

Plants in Poetry
I Had to Learn that in School

These are lines from the poems we all had to learn, and now can't forget; or did we? Let's see how well you remember these famous lines from infamous poems.

1. Longfellow shot an arrow into the air, and, of course, he lost the darn thing. But   *Long, long afterward in an _____ / I found the arrow still unbroke.*

2. Walt Whitman was an old-fashioned gardener who liked the color and charm of his rustic garden. His love for both Abraham Lincoln and the flowering shrubs he grew was immortalized in his poem,
When the _____ last in the Dooryard Bloomed.

3. James Whitcomb Riley knew that winter was fast approaching
When the frost is on the _____.

4. Longfellow wrote a poem about a husky, hardworking fellow who labored out in the open when he penned
Under the spreading _____ tree the village smithy stands.

5. Edward Lear told us about a most unlikely love affair between an owl and a pussycat who
      . . . . .sailed away for a year and a day,
      To the land where the _____ grows.

6. John Greenleaf Whittier looked back on the trials of his youth in his poem In School Days. Close your eyes and you can see that old schoolhouse still sitting by the road. There may even be a ragged beggar resting there while
      Around it still the sumacs grow,
      And the _____ vines are running.

7. Edgar Guest must have been thinking about the garden when he wrote these lines in his poem Raisin Pie
      There's a heap of pent-up goodness in the yellow bantam _____,
      And I sort o' like to linger round a _____ patch at morn;

8. Robert Loveman showed us what a wild imagination he had in his poem *April Rain*. He begins with:

> *It is not raining rain for me*
> *It's raining _____.*

In every dimpled drop he also saw wild flowers, roses and clover. He was an incurable optimist.

9. Lewis Carroll had a lot to say in *Through the Looking Glass* (*Alice in Wonderland* to Disney fans). But it was the walrus who spoke of many things,

> *Of shoes – and ships - and sealing wax*
> *Of _____ and kings –*

10. Will D. Cobb reflected on his educational memories when he wrote about student musical experiences before rock or rap. Do you remember

> *School days, School days, dear old golden rule days,*
> *Readin' and 'ritin' and 'rithmatic,*
> *Taught to the tune of a _____ stick.*

11. *In Flanders Fields* was written in 1915 by John McCrae to honor the fallen soldiers in WWI. The images are powerful and one line became a symbol for Veteran's Day.

> *In Flanders Fields the _____ blow*
> *Between the crosses, row on row,*

12. On July 30, 1918, during the Second Battle of Marne (WWI) poet Alfred Joyce Kilmer died. He left a large collection of poetry, but one of these poems almost every fifth grade school student in the latter half of the 20th century had to memorize, stand in front of the class and recite. Do you remember

> *Poems are made by fools like me,*
> *But only God can make a _____.*

Answers:
1. oak, 2. lilacs, 3. pumpkin, 4. chestnut, 5. bong tree, 6. blackberry,
7. corn, pumpkin, 8, violets, 9. cabbages, 10. hickory, 11. poppies, 12. tree

52

Sherlock Humus
and the case of the Purloined Flowers

Sherlock Humus, Plant Detective, was examining the crime scene. The vase was on its side, empty, with water covering the notes scattered on the buffet.

"I can't imagine what happened to those beautiful flowers," Lady Agnes stammered between sobs. "Herman brought them in from the yard. We have no idea what they were, and now they are gone. Who would have taken them?"

Just then Marte, the housekeeper entered the room. She was so petite she appeared hardly more than a shy gnome. All eyes turned to her. Was she an obvious suspect? How could she, a maid, have stolen the flowers and not cleaned up the spilled water? If she weren't the thief, perhaps she had some knowledge of the crime.

You can examine the clues and perhaps solve this mystery.

1. Dr. Watson, Sherlock's associate and good friend picked up a small hollow stem from the floor. "It appears to be a flute of some sort. Made from fresh wood, I would guess."

2. "Hummmm," was all Humus said as he sat it beside the soggy papers scattered on the buffet. " Look here, a handwritten note, partly blurred by the water. I believe it's a poem,"

_pril is the cruelest month, breeding
_____ out of the dead land, mixing
_emory and desire, stirring
Dull roots with spring rain.
T.S. Eliot--The Wasteland

3. Lady Agnes wiped another of the papers on the buffet with her handkerchief.
"What does this mean?" In the most minute of script is read, *Festivals abound across America. From Rochester, NY to Spokane, WA and Lombard, IL, even Mackinac Island. We shall celebrate under its branches here.*

4. Humus sniffed the air with his delicate nose. "The fragrance is haunting. It evokes images of childhood, don't you think? T'is the very scent of spring."

5. "They made such a beautiful bouquet, with their clusters of lavender and white." Lady Agnes was sobbing again.

6. "They are said to symbolize earliest love and youthful innocence," Marte spoke without lifting her eyes to meet those of the famous plant detective. She then turned and rushed from the room, clutching the tiny reed flute in her hand.

7. Soon, from the hedgerow came the faint high pitched voice of a flute. Humus gazed out the window for a few seconds then spoke, "Curious. Most curious, Watson. This gnome of a housekeeper knows more than she lets on, I suspect."

8. Watson held his fingers to his forehead, as if to better access his memory. "Legend says that Pan pursued the nymph Syrinx and turned her into a reed to make his first flute. It is from this Greek word, I suspect, that the botanical name of your bouquet was derived. Humus, is this not the *Syringia vulgarus?*"

9. "Well done, Watson." Humus was looking out the window at the footprints left in the moist earth by Marte. "You have successfully identified the flowers. See these prints?" he pointed out the window. "There are no shoes, the diminutive housekeeper was in her bare feet. One can go without shoes only after these flowers are in bloom."

10. Sherlock Humus turned his attention again to the vase and the buffet. He picked up one very small four-petaled flower. "This is the flower that the fairies make their wedding bouquets from. I am certain that we have had a wedding here today, and that your housekeeper is truly a gnome and was an attendant at this celebration of love. You know that it is said the gnomes play the flute at all fairy weddings?"

Sherlock Humus reached under the buffet and recovered something from the floor. He examined it with his magnifying glass, "Then the question is not who stole the flowers, but what we should give the fairy couple as a wedding gift."

If you haven't already solved this case the answer on page 123

It's All About Roses

The gentleman smiled when he saw them. He leaned forward and gently touched the blossom with his fingers, then inhaled the fragrance. "The thorns are sharp, and the bush itself is gangly and without aesthetic form. These leaves are the favorite dinner for every insect on six legs. They are fussy and demanding. They fall victim to molds, mildew and cold weather. Still, they are everyone's favorite flower."

Gil was a gentle man in his eighties. After spending a lifetime as a rosarian, developing new varieties of roses he was now entering Lakeview, but he was still "the Rose Man." He would share his wit and wisdom, always with a smile. There was a twinkle in his eye when he was with his roses, and when he would give a rose to a lonely lady at the dining room table. He started a rose club at Lakeview. Together staff and residents planted a rose garden. Hanging baskets filled with miniature roses hung from the gazebo. He was a great storyteller and often would sit among his friends, both the people and the roses, and share his experiences. Sometimes he would even give them a little quiz. "Just to keep 'em on their toes." he would say. This quiz is dedicated to Gil. Hope you enjoy it. After you are done take some time to smell the roses, and share some rose stories of your own.

1. FACT or FICTION   Roses are related to raspberries

2. FACT or FICTION   Rose colored glasses were invented by Benjamin Franklin.

3. FACT or FICTION   Rose hips (the fruit) are used to make a healthy tea.

4. FACT or FICTION   June is National Rose Month in the United States.

5. FACT or FICTION   Both Dolly Parton and Queen Elizabeth have roses named after them.

6. FACT or FICTION   Shakespeare never mentions the rose in any of his writing.

7. FACT or FICTION   Cleopatra carpeted the floors of her palace with rose petals when she prepared for a visit from Marc Anthony.

8. FACT or FICTION   Confucius had a 600 book library devoted to roses and their cultivation.

9. FACT or FICTION   There are no roses native to North America.

10. FACT or FICTION   David Rose was the composer of a lot of enduring music, including "The Stripper."

Do you know these famous Roses?

1. _____ Rose, a baseball player with a gambling habit.

2. _____ Rose Lee was a famous vaudeville performer.

3. Rosa _____ was a civil rights pioneer.

4. The music for "Days of Wine and Roses was written by _____ _____.

5. The _____ Rose was featured in San Francisco in 1945 during the formation of the United Nations.

Answers:
1. Fact,   2. Fiction,   3. Fact,   4. Fact,   5. Fact,   6. Fiction (he mentions the rose 50 times),
7. Fact,   8. Fact,   9. Fiction,   10. Fact

1. Pete,   2. Gypsy,   3. Parks,   4. Henry Mancini,   5. Peace

Berry Delicious

a multiple guess quiz about strawberries, springboard for discussion, taste testing

1. Strawberries are one of the very few fruits that have their seeds on the outside. The average strawberry has how many seeds?
a) 50,   b) 200,   c) 650,   d) 1200

2. "Sometimes They're Tiny, Sometimes They're Tall But Friends Are The 'Berry' Best People Of All." is a quote from what popular cartoon character?
a) Walter Knott, founder of Knott's Berry Farm
b) Halle Berry
c) NY Mets star, Darryl Strawberry
d) Strawberry Shortcake

3. *Alaska Strawberries* was a 19th century euphemism for
a) frostbitten ears
b) a rose colored quartz stone often found in gold deposits
c) dried beans
d) wooden buttons used on their heavy coats

4. The Romans used strawberries to
a) relieve depression or melancholy
b) make a glue for book binding
c) make a red toenail polish
d) sweeten sour wines

5. In the spring Bavarian farmers once tied little baskets of ripe strawberries to the horns of their cows
a) to attract the bulls
b) to attract bees so they would pollinate the apple trees
c) to keep the snakes at bay
d) as an offering to the elves to help the cows give good milk and bear healthy calves

6. Henry the VIII's second wife, Anne Boleyn, had a strawberry shaped birthmark on her neck. This was thought to make her
a) certain to bear a male heir to the throne
b) very intelligent
c) a witch
d) immune to the plague

7. Strawberry shortcake was invented by
a) German farmers
b) an unknown Spanish priest
c) Native Americans
d) Thomas Jefferson

8. Most of the world's strawberries are produced in
a) the United States
b) Russia
c) Peru
d) Canada

9. All of the following were Strawberry Shortcake's friends except
a) Raspberry Torte
b) Chocolate Drop
c) Ginger Snap
d) Plum Puddin'

10. Strawberries are closely related to
a) blueberries
b) cranberries
c) gooseberries
d) raspberries

11. In medieval folklore strawberries were served to symbolize
a) obedience
b) peace & good will
c) romantic interest in the guest
d) a need for financial assistance

12. Serving strawberries and cream is a tradition at
a) the Kentucky Derby
b) opening day of major league baseball season
c) the summer Olympics
d) the Wimbledon tennis tournament

"Doubtless God could have made a better berry, but doubtless God never did."
Dr. William Butler

Answers:

1-b, 2-d, 3-c, 4-a, 5-d, 6-c, 7-c, 8-a, 9-b, 10-d, 11-b, 12-d

Paradise Island on Your Windowsill

```
E E R T Y E N O M D S C G O D
T A P A I N E D R A G A E D I
N Q L H H P Q R I J S C R A H
A A B O I Q L N T P U T B C C
L J U Y E L O A I N M U E O R
P X A A Z G O D N U O S R V O
A R V D E Z E D I T N G D A O
R U B B E R T R E E P L A N T
B M W P P P U U M N C S I R S
E M A L L H L A L R D O S A D
Z L A R T G L A O X B R Y V I
M N S N A C H T N W N H O O F
T L A R Y D O P O T H O S N P
X M H C N N R E F N O T S O B
K W A W C A L L A L I L Y S V
```

ALOE
ANTHURIUM
AVOCADO
BEGONIA
BOSTONFERN
CACTUS
CALLALILY
CROTON
 CYCLAMEN

DRAGONTREE
GARDENIA
GERBERDAISY
HOYA
IVY
JADEPLANT
MONEYTREE
ORCHID
PALM
PHILODENDRON
POTHOS
RUBBERTREEPLANT
SPIDERPLANT
TIPLANT
ZEBRAPLANT

Ladybug, Ladybug

It was a lazy summer afternoon, that was until Michelle, the activity volunteer, showed up at The Willows. You can picture her quite easily. Young, thin, bubbly personality, talks a little too loud and treats a lot of the folks here like they was children. We hate that, but, after all, we were brought up right. We are polite. We always laughed at her jokes and agreed with what she said. She was nice so we didn't want to hurt her feelings any. That was until that crazy afternoon.

She entered the room and marched to the table where we were seated reading, coloring the pictures in the latest *Seniors Illustrated* book, or just chatting with friends. She put her blue canvas bag on the table and proclaimed at the top of her lungs so Agnes could hear, "Have I got a surprise for you this afternoon!!!" With that she pulled a mason jar from her canvas bag and held it up for us all to see.

It looked like something was crawling around inside that old jar. Claudette stood and leaned forward. "Whatcha got in there?" she shouted back.

Michelle smiled and held it closer for her to see.

"Oh my God!" she shrieked as she fell back into her chair. "It's a bunch a bugs."

"That's right," Michelle smiled. Then she held the jar out so the rest of us could see it. "Ladybugs," she continued. "Aren't they cute?"

Martha put her face almost against the glass. "Damn. You got better eyesight than I do. You sure some of them ain't gentleman bugs?"

Everyone laughed as Michelle's face turned deep red.

Claudette started singing a little song she had taught her grandchildren, "Ladybug, ladybug fly away home, your . . . . ."

Agnes cried out above the singing, "I still can't see them."

So Michelle unscrewed the lid and held it in Agnes' face. Just then about twenty of the hundred or so ladybugs decided to seek their freedom. Michelle tried to put the lid back on the jar. In the process it dropped to the table. By the time she had it right side up again, over half of the little critters had taken flight. They landed on gray hair and frail arms, eyeglasses and juice glasses.

Some of our folks screamed. Ruthie drove her wheelchair like she was running a marathon and was still screaming as she disappeared down the hall.

Grace was fascinated with the one that landed on her hand. As she turned her hand over and over she entered into a conversation with it. George was trying to help Michelle catch them and get them back in the jar. Soon several others joined in the effort. Carlos and Matilde came running into the room. They immediately grasped what was happening. They would have helped, but they were too busy laughing.

Within minutes half of the staff was in the room along with Doreen Manchester, the administrator. Many insisted that this was the first time they had ever seen her laugh. But her laughter was contagious. Soon the screaming had stopped and the laughter took over.

Every time someone caught one of these little critters and Michelle opened the jar to put it in, two or three more would escape. Maryann said it was like trying to put toothpaste back in the tube.

Doreen asked Michelle what they ate, but Michelle didn't know. Doreen then turned and walked out the door, leaving all the confusion behind. But, in a few minutes she returned with two paper plates. One had pieces of apple and watermelon on it. The other had vanilla and chocolate ice cream. She sat the plates on the table but not a single lady bug came to the party, although George did grab a couple pieces of watermelon when he thought no one was looking.

It was George who finally went over and opened the windows. Most found their way to the shrubbery and flowers outside. But a few stayed and visited for the rest of the afternoon.

Carlos said, "I think they eat other bugs, like aphids and such." He went outside and soon returned with a handful of weeds and a couple dahlias. "Don't want them to starve just because they came to visit," he commented as he filled a vase with water and arranged the weeds. "These got aphids on 'em."

About a dozen of these ladybugs decided to stay and every afternoon, Carlos would bring fresh weeds and discard the ones that were beyond their prime.

Martha was the one that noticed the tiny orange eggs under the pigweed leaf. A few minutes at the computer and she declared "We're gonna have babies."

"Speak for yourself," Claudette responded. "None of this WE stuff."

Now a magnifying glass stayed on the table beside the vase. It became a ritual. Every time someone came into the room they would go over to the vase and take a look at the eggs. In about two weeks they began to hatch into little black and orange larvae with a voracious appetite. Now it was important to feed these "kids." Even if they were "ugly as sin."

As the days got shorter and the nights a little colder it was agreed that the ladybug population would move out to the rose garden. Before that happened, Cam Williams took a bunch of photos, real closeups, of the adults and the kids. Some of them still hang in the lobby. When you stop by for a visit, remind me and I'll show 'em to you.

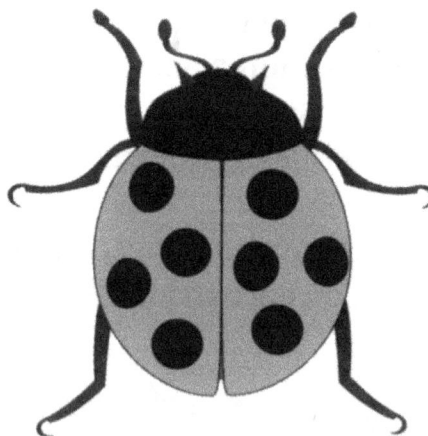

Uninvited Guests in the Garden

There are a lot of uninvited guests found in the garden. While many are welcome, others aren't. You decide which of the following would be welcome in your garden. Some might welcome a given critter while in another garden they might not be considered a friend. As we go down this garden path and discover these visitors, there might be many opportunities for conversation, story swapping and perhaps a good joke or two.

1. Mr. Toad   WELCOME or UNWELCOME

2. Honey Bee   WELCOME or UNWELCOME

3. Hummingbird   WELCOME or UNWELCOME

4. Robin   WELCOME or UNWELCOME

5. Earthworm   WELCOME or UNWELCOME

6. Grasshopper   WELCOME or UNWELCOME

7. Ladybug   WELCOME or UNWELCOME

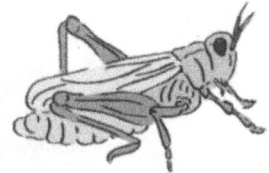

8. Rabbit   WELCOME or UNWELCOME

9. Praying Mantis WELCOME or UNWELCOME

10. Orb Spider   WELCOME or UNWELCOME

11. Box Turtle   WELCOME or UNWELCOME

12. Wren   WELCOME or UNWELCOME

13. Ragweed   WELCOME or UNWELCOME

14. Snails   WELCOME or UNWELCOME

15. Gopher   WELCOME or UNWELCOME

16. Dandelion   WELCOME or UNWELCOME

17. Butterfly   WELCOME or UNWELCOME

18. Aphids   WELCOME or UNWELCOME

19. Spot, the   WELCOME or UNWELCOME
Neighbor's Dog

20. Grandchildren WELCOME or UNWELCOME

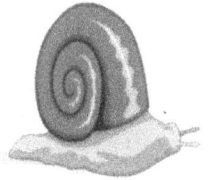

Answers:
1-W, 2-W, 3-W, 4-W, 5.-W, 6-U, 7-W, 8-U, 9-W, 10-W, 11-W, 12-W,
13-U, 14-U, 15-U, 16-W or U, 17-W or U, 18-U, 19-W or U, 20-W

Watermelon Whimsy

Watermelons are grown and enjoyed all over the world. Let's see how well you know this delightful summer treat. If you can get five of these questions right, you have earned a slice of watermelon.

1. FACT or FICTION   During the Civil War Confederate soldiers boiled watermelons to make a sweet syrup.

2. FACT or FICTION   Watermelons originated in China.

3. FACT or FICTION   The Russians enjoy a watermelon beer.

4. FACT or FICTION   Watermelon rind can be made into pickles.

5. FACT or FICTION   Agua de Sandia is a Mexican cold drink made with watermelons and limes.

6. FACT or FICTION   The United States is the world's largest producer of watermelons.

7. FACT or FICTION   The average American eats between 15 and 20 pounds of watermelon a year.

8. FACT or FICTION   Watermelon is about 98% water.

9. FACT or FICTION   While the watermelon is cool and refreshing there in no nutritional value in it.

10. FACT or FICTION   There are both red and yellow fleshed watermelons.

11. FACT or FICTION   The world record for watermelon seed-spitting is 66'11", held by Jack Dietz of Chicago.

12. FACT or FICTION   Watermelon carving contests have become a part of many 4th of July celebrations.

Answers:
1. Fact, 2. Fiction, 3. Fact, 4. Fact, 5. Fact, 6. Fiction, 7. Fact,
8. Fact, 9. Fiction, 10. Fact, 11. Fact,. 12. Fact.

Watermelon Feast

As we sit here in our study looking out the window, beyond the garden we can see the mountain that dominates the Albuquerque landscape. Sandia Mountain, translated from the Spanish, is "Watermelon Mountain." This is because of the delightful red color of this mountain for a few minutes almost every sunset. Locally it is referred to as "red mountain time."

Last year several of the Native American communities here engaged in a Great Watermelon Contest. The goal was to grow the largest watermelon, the sweetest watermelon, or the ugliest watermelon. A tribal senior center even held a Watermelon feast with lots of watermelon to share.

There was watermelon carving, much more artistic than simple carving a face in a pumpkin. They made their watermelons a work of art. The layers of color, green, white and red truly enhance the creative opportunities

They also held a watermelon seed spitting contest and a rind chucking contest.

But the high point of the feast was the food. Every dish had to have watermelon as one of the ingredients. Some were delightful, some were memorable, some were of questionable culinary value. But the recipes were shared and someone came up with a country western song about a watermelon moon.

Your community, neighborhood, or family, can host your own Watermelon Feast and unleash your creativity. Let us know about the high points of your feast.

Tomato Soup, a Quiz

The tomato is America's favorite vegetable. Yes, we know, technically, it's a fruit. Regardless of what you call it, it's Number One. In a program we did once, we polled the audience on their favorite way to eat tomatoes. "In a pizza sauce" was by far the first choice. A very close second was "In a salad." Other votes were cast for tomato juice, salsa, ketchup, fresh from the garden and in a Bloody Mary. Perhaps it's because this is such a versatile vegetable (fruit for you purists) that it is our national favorite. Perhaps it's because it tastes good, or is easy to grow. Or is it because it is good for us? No, that couldn't be it.

Whether you like your tomatoes juiced, on a Big Mac or in a soup, we thought you might enjoy a little quiz about this delightful food. Let's see how well you know the main ingredient in spaghetti sauce.

1. TRUE or FALSE. The tomato originated in Italy.

2. The tomato is first cousin to:
(a) tobacco, (b) chile peppers, (c) deadly nightshade, (d) all of the above, (e) none of these

3. The first president to grow tomatoes for the table was:
(a) George Washington, (b) Thomas Jefferson, (c) Abraham Lincoln, (d) Theodore Roosevelt, (e) Millard Fillmore

4. The average American eats ___ pounds of processed tomatoes each year:
(a) 25,   (b) 54,   (c) 73,   (d) 107,   (e) 133

5. The community of Bunol in Spain celebrates the world's largest food fight every August. For an hour thousands of people throw thousands of pounds of tomatoes at each other and assorted other targets. What is this festival called?
(a) Festival La Tomatina, (b) Salsa Street Party, (c) Dia Del Loco Tomatillo

6. TRUE or FALSE Tomatoes were long thought to be poisonous.

7. TRUE or FALSE Tomatoes are a great source of Vitamin C.

8. TRUE or FALSE   Tomatoes in tin cans were one of the rations provided to both Union and Confederate troops during the Civil War.

9. When the tomato was first introduced to France it was called the:
(a) Stinking apple, (b) Moor's apple, (c) Love apple, (d) Spanish apple.

10. The German name for the tomato inspired its botanical name, *Lycopersicon esculentum*. A translation of the German name means:
(a) Vine with edible fruit, (b) Bitter fruit, (c) Red heart vine, (d) edible wolf peach

Answers to Tomato Soup

1. FALSE, the tomato is native to South America and the Caribbean. It was introduced to Europe by the Spanish in the 1500's where it became a hit in Seville, because it blended so well with olive oil and garlic.

2. (d) all of the above. Tobacco, chile peppers, sweet peppers, eggplant and many popular flowering annuals are in the same family as the tomato. This Solanaceae family also hosts nightshade, belladonna and Jimson weed.

3. (b) Thomas Jefferson

4. (c) 73 pounds of processed tomatoes annually, and you can add to that 19 pounds of fresh tomatoes for every man, women and child in the United States.

5. (a) Festival La Tomatina. This festival began in the days of Franco. One source states that the tomatoes were aimed at local politicians. Today it is more of a tourist attraction as a quarter of a million pounds of tomatoes are dumped onto the streets and everyone becomes a target. After one hour of a food fight unrivaled anywhere else in the world everyone hits the showers and high pressure hoses clean the streets.

6. TRUE, the tomato is in the same family as deadly nightshade. Plants, like people are judged by the company they keep, so the tomato was suspect. Still the Spanish, Italians and French appreciated the tomato soon after its introduction to Europe. Spain decreed that tomatoes be planted at all ports of call to provide fruit for their sailors. The incidence of scurvy was much lower on Spanish ships than the English and Dutch. It should be noted that the leaves are toxic and should not be eaten. They contain solanine (a Glycoalkaloid) that can cause severe gastric distress, hallucinations, loss of body functioning and even death.

7. TRUE, tomatoes are very nutritious. Vitamins A & C, iron and lycopene all make this one of those rare combinations of a food that both tastes good and is good for you.

8. TRUE, the canned tomato was a popular part of field rations for both sides. Military campsites often accumulated large garbage dumps filled with empty tin cans. Foods preserved in tin cans were a popular way to store and transport provisions for an army on the march from the Napoleonic expeditions until today.

9. (c) It was called the love apple because of a firm conviction that dining on this fruit could inspire romance. This was in part due to the fact that the bright red fruit symbolized the heart, hence true love. There was a poem written in the mid 1600's that described the tomato as being just like love, delicious, beautiful, and dangerous.

10. (d) It may have been called "wolf peach" because of the hairy leaves that some thought resembled a wolf's ear. Of course the fruit itself does resemble a peach. Carolus Linnaeus adapted this common name when he assigned the botanical nomenclature Lycopersicon esculentum.

Under an Assumed Name

1. Before it was a Raisin it was a _____ .

2. Before it was cider it was _____ .

3. Before it was a pickle it was a _____ .

4. Before it was saurkraut it was _____ .

5. Before it was a prune it was a _____ .

6. Before it was Tequila it was an _____ .

7. Before it was a French Fry it was a _____ .

8. Before it was Borsch it was a _____ .

9. Before it was Polenta it was _____ .

10. Before it was coriander it was _____ .

11. Before it was guacamole is was an _____ .

12. Before it was catsup it was a _____ .

What Part of the Plant Are You Eating?

A matching quiz springboard for tasting & discussion

1. ___ Asparagus

2. ___ Broccoli

3. ___ Yams

4. ___ Peanuts

5. ___ Watermelon

6. ___ Celery

7. ___ Carrots

8. ___ Corn

9. ___ Lima Beans

10. ___ Artichoke

11. ___ Ginger

12. ___ Radish

13. ___ Beet

14. ___ Spinach

15. ___ Peach

16. ___ Pumpkin

17. ___ Zucchini

18. ___ Rhubarb

19. ___ Dates

20. ___ Saffron

A. Seeds

B. Flowers

C. Leaves

D. Stems

E. Roots

F. Fruit

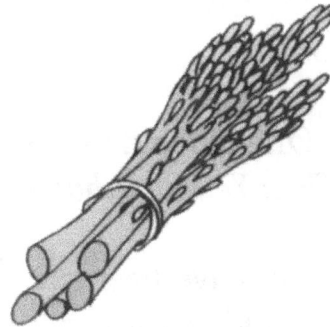

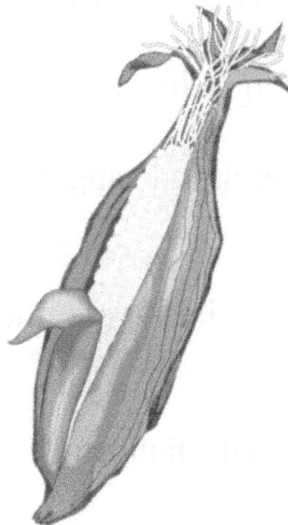

Answers:
1-D,   2-B,   3-E,   4-A,   5-F,   6-D,
7-E,   8-A,   9-A,   10-B,   11-E,   12-E,
13-E,   14-C,   15-F,   16-F,   17-F,
18-D,   19-F,   20-B

Singing in the Garden

We sing songs of romance sought, found and lost with flowers as the metaphor. We also find flowers, fruit, trees and even an occasional weed lurking in the lyrics of popular music. The following little quiz is to test your memory of songs from yesteryears. If you have an irresistible urge to burst into song, that's ok. If stories come to mind, share them. This is a great group quiz, cooperation counts, and everyone wins.

1. Nat King Cole sang of the _____ *Rose* as a musical metaphor.

2. Tony Orlando and the Dawn sang a song of hope when they asked a loved one to *Tie a Yellow Ribbon 'round the* _____ _____ _____.

3. The Irish have been particularly enthusiastic about roses with even more classics including the beautiful ballad, *The Banks of the Roses*. They also gave us *To a* ____ *Rose* and *My* ____ *Irish Rose*.

4. Who can forget the great country western song _____ _____ *Special*.

5. Barbara Streisand sang about a lady from Second Avenue called _____ _____ ____.

6. Henry Mancini wrote the award winning classic *Days of Wine and* _____.

7. Then there's the famous Beatles song _____ *Fields Forever*.

8. We can fast forward to the hard rock of Guns & Roses and their album,_____*Roses*.

9. *A White Sports Coat and a Pink* _____ became the musical trademark of Marty Robbins

10. Neil Diamond gave us _____ Rosie.

11. Of course, every child knows that *Mares eat* _____ *and Does eat* ____ *and little Lambs eat* _____ .

12. Who can forget Ricky Nelson's _____ *Party?*

13. Ann Ronell wrote _____ *Weep for Me*, a song made famous by everyone from Frank Sinatra to Louis Armstrong.

14. John Denver sang a delightful song about *Home Grown* _____ .

15. David Mallett wrote the lyrics to the song John Denver called a metaphor for life itself when he planted a row inch by inch in the _____ *Song*

Historical Plants

The history of the world is rich with references to plants that have played a role in the progress of Humanity. Dust off those old history books and see if you can fill in the blanks in this little quiz. Unlike seventh grade history tests, it's ok to share answers with your neighbor. You might think of a few we have missed. If so let us know. It may end up in the next collection in this series.

1. The _____ was named in honor of the Cherokee leader who created an alphabet.

2. The _____ Tree in Boston played an important part in the Revolutionary War.

3. The _____ tree is so tough that it became the nickname of Andrew Jackson.

4. George Washington's first experience in the timber industry of colonial America was a disaster. As his first logging job he is said to have cut down his father's _____ _____.

5. Socrates was sentenced to death by drinking tea. This was a special tea brewed from the leaves of _____, not the tree, but a member of the carrot family.

6. A wandering itinerant preacher named John Chapman roamed the Ohio frontier planting _____ trees and seeds.

7. The winners of the early Olympic games in Greece were given crowns of _____ branches.

8. A famous costume party was held in Boston in 1772. _____ was the center of attraction at this rather rowdy event.

9. King John signed a very important British document under the tree that became known as the Charter _____.

10. A poem written by a Canadian doctor, John McCrae, immortalized the red _____ that grew on the battlefield and burial sites of that Allied soldiers fallen at what is known as Flanders Field in France.

11. The bald eagle symbol of the United States carries in its talons arrows and an _____ branch.

12. The Mexican flag shows a golden eagle devouring a rattlesnake while perched on a _____.

13. You know that spring has arrived when the _____ _____ blossom in Washington, DC.

14. Robin Hood and his band made the famous English Long Bow from the _____.

15. The floral symbol of Scotland is the _____.

16. The maple leaf appears on the flag of _____.

17. According to the Book of Genesis the first clothing was made from _____ _____.

18. In Nova, Ohio the last remaining tree planted by this true American hero still grows and still bears fruit. It was planted by _____ _____.

19. A horse chestnut tree is still growing in Amsterdam. It is now at least 150 years old, but it was a beautiful tree during World War II. This tree is famous because it was immortalized in
a) General Eisenhower's journal,
b) in a photograph of an end-of-the-war celebration,
c) A WWII movie staring John Wayne,
d) Anne Frank's diary.

20. The Joshua tree, a variety of yucca, seen so often in the era of western movies was named by . . .
a) Roy Rogers,
b) a group of Mormans when they crossed the Mojave Desert,
c) a Spanish frier when California was being colonized,
d) Zane Gray when he wrote one of his earlier western novels.

Answers:
1. Sequoia, 2. Liberty, 3. Hickory, 4. Cherry Tree, 5. Poison Hemlock, 6. Apple, 7. Laurel, 8. Tea, 9. Oak, 10. Poppies, 11. Olive, 12. Cactus, 13. Cherry trees, 14. Yew, 15. Thistle, 16. Canada, 17. Fig leaves, 18. Johnny Appleseed (or John Chapman), 19-d, 20-b

Tools of the Trade

The art of gardening requires both the right attitude
and the right tools.

```
Q W Z R R S R X K D L C S S H
R P H E Y E H N D E K U P M C
C E G E N S E O A G T L R I N
F D D U E E O F V I X T I L E
E C R E P L B L L E P I N E B
T P Z A E L B L W I L V K S X
R P D Y O W E A L N F A L R S
I S H W G R X M R A H T E A E
A O S H E A R S R N O R K V
H R E T S O P M O C O R S E O
C R A I N G A U G E S W U E L
N T A H W A R T S P A D E O G
W Y K H X L E W O R T L P D J
A U O Q O T X W O Z Q J B N Z
L E X F W A T E R I N G C A N
```

BENCH
COMPOSTER
CULTIVATOR
EDGER
GLOVES
HOE
HOSE
JOURNAL

KNEEPADS
LAWN CHAIR
LEAF BLOWER
PRUNER
RAIN GAUGE
RAKE
SHEARS
SHOVEL
SMILES

SPADE
SPRINKLER
STRAW HAT
TILLER
TROWEL
WATERING CAN
WEEDER
WHEELBARROW

Growing Laughter in the Garden

Too often we focus on the work, the drudgery and the self imposed stress of gardening. But gardening isn't a somber activity. Truth is, most of us plant people have a great sense of humor. The real value of our people-plant connection is often found in that humor. *New gardeners learn by trowel and error.*

Many of us can relate to Buddy Hackett's famous comment; *My mother's menu consisted of two choices: Take it or leave it.*

Sometimes it's silly stuff that we can share with a child. Like the ageless riddle, *What did Santa Claus say when he walked through a garden?*
Hoe! Hoe! Hoe!

And sometimes the humor is a little more profound. *I garden, therefore I weed.*

The following are some jokes planted in the garden in an attempt to harvest a smile, a chuckle or perhaps a belly laugh. But, the joke's on you. The catch is you have to furnish the punch line. We have provided the popular answers, but strongly suspect that you can do even better. Good luck.

1. Like a prune, you are not getting any better looking, but you are getting _____. - *N. D. Stice*

2. Research tells us twelve out of every ten individuals like _____.

3. God made rainy days, so gardeners could get ___ _____ _____.

4. If you're a gardener you might call yourself a "plant _____."

5. Lassie, a famous garden dog wants to know, "What do you get if you cross a dog with a daisy?" _____.

6. What do you call it when worms take over the world? _____ _____.

7. A toddler was found chewing on a slug.
After the initial surge of disgust the parent said,
"Well . . . What does it taste like?"
"_____," was the reply.

8. Knowledge is knowing a tomato is a fruit; Wisdom is not putting it in a _____
_____.

9. While Leo Tolstoy was writing his great novel, his gardener was also working on a somewhat lesser known literary work titled "War and _____."

10. Some potatoes are just like people. They never seem motivated to participate, but are content to watch others work and play. They are called "_____."

11. A weed is a plant that has mastered every survival skill except for _____ according to Doug Larson.

12. A woman's garden is growing beautifully but the darn tomatoes won't ripen. There's a limit to the number of uses for green tomatoes and she's getting tired of it. So she goes to her neighbor and says, "Your tomatoes are ripe, mine are green. What can I do about it?'"

Her neighbor replies, "Well, it may sound absurd but here's what to do. Tonight there's no moon. After dark go out into your garden and take all your clothes off. Tomatoes can see in the dark and they'll be embarrassed and blush. In the morning they'll all be red, you'll see."

Well, what the heck? She does it. The next day her neighbor asks how it worked. "So-so," she answers, "The tomatoes are still green but _____."

Answers:
1. Sweeter,   2. Chocolate,   3. The housework done,   4. manager,   5. A collie-flower,
6. Global Worming,   7. Worms,   8. fruit salad,   9. Peas,   10. Speck Tators ,
11. learning to grow in rows,   12. the cucumbers are all four inches longer

El Coco,
The Bogeyman's Hiding Under the Bed

The coconut is one of the most popular foods in the world and it's the most widely grown palm. This symbol of the tropics provides a nutritious fruit and a flavorful liquid called coconut water. It's the source of a valuable oil used in food preparation, soaps, shampoo, cosmetics and even the manufacturing of paints.

During a horticultural therapy session several years back we were passing around some sensory items. Among them was a hairy old coconut with the three indentations that looked for all the world like a monkey face.

Amanda, one of the ladies in the gathering, started laughing when this fruit reached her hands. We asked her if she knew a good story about coconuts that she could share with the rest of us.

"Si," she said, "I am from the Philippines and my father grew many coconuts. When I was a just a nina, I was misbehaving and my father told me that El Coco, that's what we called the Bogeyman, would get me if I didn't go to bed and stay there all night."

Everyone looked puzzled. Finally another lady asked "Where did this El Coco hide?"

Amanda smiled, "Why, under my bed of course. Even today I can recall how it felt."

Others in the room gasped. Was there really a bogeyman, El Coco?

"It was long after all had gone to bed. I needed to pee. I was afraid that El Coco was hiding, waiting for me to step on the floor. Then he would grab my ankles, drag me under the bed and eat me."

"What did you do?" several others asked at once.

"I carefully reached down with my hand and felt under my bed. Just when I thought I was safe I felt this furry head, then I felt its eye. I screamed. As loud as I could, I screamed. In the process I wet my bed. A lot!"

"Papa came running in, but not to save me. No. He was laughing. I pointed under my bed but was too scared to speak. He got down on his knees and reached under the bed. I thought for a moment how brave my papa was. Then he held the coconut up into the bright moonlight and started laughing at me again."

"What happened next?" the activity director wanted to know.

"Next I laughed because Mama made him change my bedding."

"So it was the coconut that gave a face to the old Bogeyman," one of the others responded. "I thought it was like that nasty little demon the Chucacabra, the goat-sucker, so popular where I grew up in Puerto Rico."

This led into another lengthy conversation where everyone was getting involved with their own versions of the Bogeyman and both humorous and scary stories that had to be shared. We never did get beyond the coconuts as this conversation continued until the dining room was opened for lunch. These folks never got to the little quiz that follows, but WOW! We all learned a lot, and their discussion was a lot more entertaining than what we had to say. Sometimes it pays to simply let go and let the conversation flow.

When your group is sufficiently diverse, and comfortable enough to share stories, it can be well worth listening.

The Remarkable Coconut, a Quiz

1. TRUE or FALSE. The liquid inside an immature coconut is sterile and contains a natural sugar, making it a healthy refreshing drink.

2. TRUE of FALSE. During various conflicts in the tropics coconut shells have been filled with gunpowder and used like grenades.

3. TRUE or FALSE. The rescue of the crew from the PT109 was possible when a coast watcher found a message etched in a coconut, then set adrift. So we owe the presidency of JFK to a coconut.

4. TRUE or FALSE. Coconut husks have been used to make cigarette filters.

5. TRUE or FALSE. The Foley Sound Effects system used in the movies used coconut shells to produce the sound of horses' hoof beats.

6. TRUE or FALSE. Sap from the fruiting stem of the coconut is used to produce an alcoholic beverage called *arrack*.

7. TRUE or FALSE. Coconut trunks have been hollowed out to make canoes.

8. TRUE or FALSE. Coconut oil has been used as a substitute for diesel fuel.

9. TRUE or FALSE. Copra, the dried flesh of the coconut is the source of cocaine.

10. TRUE or FALSE. One of the rarest gemstones in the world is the famous "coconut pearl" which forms within the wall of a coconut shell.

11. TRUE or FALSE. The flesh of a young coconut is gelatinous and is called "coconut slime."

12. TRUE or FALSE. Because coconuts float they have been found as far from the tropics as the coast of Norway.

One of the greatest all time projects taken on by an adult day care center happened when one of the gentlemen brought in a ripe coconut in the husk. They planted it in sand in a leaky children's swimming pool. Half buried in the sand it sprouted in about three months and is now seven years old.

Answers:

1. TRUE, In fact, this coconut water, or milk, was used by field surgeons during WWII as an intravenous glucose solution when the medical preparation wasn't available.

2. TRUE, This was a common weapon of mass destruction in many of independence movements in the tropics and was used by both sides during WWII.

3. TRUE, and that coconut is on display at the John F. Kennedy Library now.

4. TRUE, the husk is burned without oxygen to produce porous activated charcoal that is used in the production of some gas masks, cigarette filters, aquarium filters, and filters to remove radioactive particles in the air at nuclear power plants.

5. TRUE, When used in various mediums, like sand, pebbles or wood, different sounds could be produced in the studio.

6. TRUE, this sweet sap is used to produce a coarse sugar, wine, vinegar and coconut beer. When fermented and distilled, the alcoholic beverage is called Arrack.

7. TRUE. The trunk is also cut into lumber for building, furniture and fence posts.

8. TRUE. During WWII, and since then, in many parts of the tropics coconut oil has been used when diesel wasn't available.

9. FALSE, copra is the dried flesh of the coconut and is used as food, the source of coconut oil, and to manufacture cosmetics, medicines and many food items ranging from ice cream to cookies, but not cocaine.

10. Maybe TRUE, maybe FALSE. There is no scientific proof of a coconut producing a pearl and there is nothing within the coconut that matches the chemical composition of a pearl. Yet, there are collectors of rare and exotic gem stones that claim to have the incredibly rare coconut pearl.

11. FALSE, the contents of the young coconut is called "coconut jelly" and is considered delicious and sweet.

12. TRUE, in fact there are records of one being sprouted and grown in a greenhouse for many years after being rescued from a Norwegian beach.

Strolling Down Autumn Lane

Courtney was always doing something that was going to get her into trouble, her and anyone nearby. It started one Wednesday afternoon when she decided she'd had enough Bingo. She grabbed a canvas shopping bag and a pair of scissors and waltzed out the door. In about an hour she returned and headed straight to the activity room.

She spread her new found treasures out on the table by the window. After filling a number of empty jars, coffee mugs and anything else that would hold water she soon had a display somewhere between clutter and art. Her collection of flowers, leaves and other assorted finds covered the table. She took the old "Game of Life" board from the closet and used it as a pattern as she turned the craft paper on the table into a huge game board with a circular path, with her harvest of treasures distributed along the way.

Next she made up the score card with the names of each flower, leaf or treasure she had found. You had to roll the dice and move around the curving pathway. When you landed on one of these autumn treasures, you could check it off your card. The first one to complete the card was the winner.

These are some of the treasures she found along her Autumn Lane. You will find a completely different collection of treasures depending upon where you live.

Goldenrod

Milkweed pods

Acorns

Fall asters

Sugar maple leaves

White oak leaves

A green and yellow gourd

Zinnias

Marigolds

A large sunflower

Plume of Pampas grass

Her Autumn Lane Game became so popular with the other residents that it was enlarged and moved to the courtyard, with discoveries at every turn.

Everyone took turns strolling down their own Autumn lane, making their own discoveries. Sometimes they would take short hikes of discovery around the neighborhood.

Sometimes discoveries were made that they couldn't identify. But they had a lot of fun trying to find out. Some would go to the library, others to their computers.

When the weather wasn't cooperating they continued to play the table game using both real items and photos. Conversation continued to flow and memories continued to be triggered.

During one of the outdoor strolls down the street, one of the gentlemen began picking up the soda cans, paper and plastic bags that littered the streets and paths. This soon became a part of the adventure. Those participating in the "Policing" were awarded official blue plastic gloves to use.

The next spring found several of these folks out along their "lane" planting flowers for others to discover as the seasons continued their cycle.

Share your thoughts and opinions about the harvest season and a little journey down your own Autumn Lane. You can even work together to create your own Autumn Lane Game.

From Pumpkins to Jack-O-Lanterns

Pumpkins fascinate us. Glen, a resident of the Oak Hill Senior Center, was talking with a group of children who were visiting the week before Halloween. They had come to paint faces on pumpkins, but it soon became obvious that they knew absolutely nothing about this remarkable fruit/vegetable. They knew that they are big, and that they become almost human when we carve or paint faces on them. Many of these children hadn't even made the connection between the pumpkin sitting before them and the pumpkin pie on the dinner table.

This bothered Glen, a farmer in past years, now the unofficial "Gardener of Oak Hill." He stood and asked all the children, the other Oak Hill residents, and the staff to follow him out the side door. That's where the children were introduced to the collection of raised beds that were the Oak Hill Vegetable Patch. He suggested that these children find their own pumpkins to decorate.

While they were searching he began firing questions at them. Soon all the other residents attending this intergenerational Pumpkin Party were quizzing the children too. The following are from the questions they asked. Let's see how well you can do with their little quiz.

1. Before they approached the garden Glen held up his hand, "How do pumpkins grow?"
a) on trees, b) on vines, c) on bushes, d) underground

2. "Who can be the first to find a pumpkin blossom?" Beatrice asked. One of the children fired back, "What color flower are we looking for?" Beatrice answered
a) White, b) pink, c) pale blue, d) orange

3. While they were looking, Glen decided to test their literary knowledge. "What poet wrote '*When the frost is on the punkin, and the fodder's in the shock . . . .?*' Their guesses included the following. Do you know who was right?
a) James Whitcome Riley, b) Robert Frost, c) Mickey Mouse, d) Dora the Explorer

4. Margie, one of the ladies present, had been a elementary teacher before her retirement. She asked, "Which Disney princess rode to the ball in a carriage made out of a pumpkin?
a) Sleeping Beauty, b) Snow White, c) Cinderella, d) Pocahontas

5. Glen was pleased when one of the children returned with a large pumpkin flower and asked him, "Where do pumpkins come from?" Do you know which of these answers is correct?
a) Europe, b) Asia, c) The Americas, d) Africa, e) Australia

6. Luisa asked, "In Mexico City, when I was a little girl, we ate pepitas. Do you know what pepitas are?" One of these guesses was correct. Do you know which one?
a) Pumpkin seeds, b) Fried pumpkin flowers, c) Pumpkin candy
d) Pumpkin shaped cookies

7. Orin was the activity program volunteer. He laughed out loud as the children discovered the pumpkins and chose their own fruit to make into Jack-O-Lanterns. "Do you know what they used to carve in Europe before they discovered pumpkins?" There were puzzled looks on the faces of the children, and some of the seniors. Their guesses included all of the following, but only one of them is correct.
a) Apples, b) turnips, c) potatoes, d) coconuts, e) cabbages

8. One of the children turned the tables on their grandfriends as they returned to the activity room with pumpkins in hand. Glen was showing them how we used to carve pumpkins rather than paint faces on them. Alex snickered and asked, "Do you know what we call the insides of a pumpkin?" The guesses the elders made included; the guts, yucky stuff, pumpkin slime and brains. As a child, did you have a nickname for the pumpkin's insides?

9. Michelle's eyes were focused on the pumpkin pies sitting on the other table. She came up with a question of her own. "Who invented pumpkin pie?" Both the seniors and the kids made guesses on this, but only one of them was right. Which one?
a) The French chefs in Paris, b) The Native Americans, c) Ben Franklin
d) Thomas Jefferson, e) Aunt Libby

10. While the children were painting scary, funny and really weird faces on their pumpkins, Glen asked one more pumpkin question. "Do you know what percentage of the pumpkins produced in the United States becomes Jack-O-Lanterns?" One of the guesses below is correct. Do you know which one?
a) 15%, b) 35%, c) 60%, d) 90%

answers on next page

Conversations in the pumpkin patch

Pumpkins have been called the fun food of the American garden but they far more than toys. Pumpkins are very nutritious and can be enjoyed in many more ways than simply a pie. Do you have a favorite, other than pie, way to eat pumpkins? Got a good recipe you would like to share?

Lakewood's garden club grew a fabulous crop of pumpkins and made them into vases to hold a bouquet of wild flowers. These were than placed on the tables in the dining room. Note: this is a short term project because in about two days the pumpkin begins to spoil. But it's whimsical beauty for the moment.

Grace and Joshua round up pumpkins from their neighborhood every November first and take them to a local homeless shelter, along with some of their favorite recipes.

In Millsboro, DE they hold an annual World Championship Punkin Chunkin' Festival where they use catapults to toss pumpkins.

We were told that one community used to host a Pumpkin Shoot to raise funds for a local conservation project.

Answers to the Pumpkin Quiz:
1-b, 2-d, 3-a, 4-c, 5-c, 6-a, 7-b,
8 - Whatever you answer is right.
9-b, 10-c (This can vary from location to location, but the average is 60-70%)

Sherlock Humus
and Case of the Mysterious Odor

Dame Elizabeth held the smelling salts to her nose again, then dabbed her cheeks with the embroidered handkerchief. "I don't know what it is, and, and, OH! I'm feeling faint again."

Dr. Watson helped her to the settee, then motioned for the maid to bring a cup of tea.

Sherlock Humus, the world famous plant detective, was feeling a bit out of his element here. It was purely by accident that he happened to be on Cobblestone Court. The gardener, an old friend, had called on him to identify a bulb that had decided to burst forth into bloom for the first time ever.

He paced the room, utilizing his rather prominent nose to assess the various household scents and seasonal aromas. He detected what he thought might be the offensive odor when he neared the door to the kitchen. Although he thought it rather familiar, a scent that tugged at his memory, he couldn't identify it until he entered the kitchen.

"Yes! Yes! That's it." Dame Elizabeth gasped as she sat up to accept her cup of tea. "It has to be something spicy they have used in the preparation of the food for my party this afternoon. Ohhh. This is horrible. I can't serve something like this to my guests. After all, they are British. The most expressive seasoning we use is butter and, perhaps, salt in moderation." She slumped back into the padded brocade chair.

Humus listened intently, not to Dame Elizabeth but to the voices in the kitchen. He entered the chef's quarters as Dr. Watson helped Dame Elizabeth to the conservatory to escape the offending odor.

The moment he entered the chef's domain he had the mystery solved. With a smile on his face he mustered his best Italian "Bon journo," he said as he lifted the lid from one of the pots. "Ahhh!" he exclaimed as he sampled the sauce bubbling before him, "Magnifico." Then he paused. The smile became a frown. "I fear that Dame Elizabeth is unaccustomed to the richness of your cuisine."

"But, boun amico, she requested our services for this party. It is to be a celebration of the arts of Rome. And, are we not artists as well?"

Sherlock assessed the work table and picked up a couple of the items sitting there. "I think I may be able to help."

He stepped outside and asked the gardener to collect for him at least six mosquitoes and put them in a jar with a lid so they could not escape. As he reentered the house he paused at the small wall hanging in the parlor. It was a papyrus with a scene of the pyramids on it. One of those inexpensive trinkets for the tourists visiting Cairo to be sure, but it was still a genuine papyrus.

He collected several other items as he made his way to the conservatory. "I have solved your mystery for you. And now I will present the clues and see how quickly you can resolve the source of the odor you find so disagreeable.

1. He held out the papyrus, "The builders of the pyramids paid their laborers, not with coin, but with the bulbs of a fragrant lily." Dame Elizabeth and Dr. Watson looked at him with puzzled expressions.

2. "The Romans, to whom you are dedicating your event this evening, dedicated the source of your offensive odor to Mars, the god of war."

3. When there was no response he continued, "During the Middle Ages most of Europe used this as the first line of defense against the Bubonic Plague, also known as the Black Death."

Dame Elizabeth gasped and clutched her throat at the mention of this horrible epidemic. But still the clues meant nothing to her.

4. Just then the gardener entered the room carrying a large glass jar buzzing with mosquitoes. While the gardener cautiously opened jar, Humus broke apart the bulb he held in his hand and quickly dropped one of the bruised segments among the angry insects. Within seconds they were clustered at the top of the jar, desperate to escape.

Watson scowled, but still the identity escaped him. Dame Elizabeth was feeling faint again and was not amused by his parlor trick.

5. Humus continued with his clues. "The juice of this seasoning you dislike was often called Russian penicillin because it was used to treat wounded soldiers during conflict."

6. "Have you encountered any vampires on this beautiful estate?" Humus asked. She appeared almost angry. "Of course not," was her shocked reply.

7. "It may be because of the number of wild cousins of this popular herb growing around your home here." He smiled as he made this last statement, then help up a sample of the native botanical relative. "They are said to keep vampires at bay."

8. "In the past, it was the habit of fairies and other little people to snatch babies from cradles. But a braid of these bulbs was hung on the head of the cradle to keep them away and keep the infant safe." Humus continued.

Dr. Watson smiled broadly at this. His research into the mythology of the British Isles now served him well. He now knew the identity of the source of this mysterious odor. Dame Elizabeth was still in a quandary.

9. Sherlock Humus held up a strange metal tool. "This is used to extract the juice from the segments of this bulb. Incidently, these segments are referred to as cloves, although they have no connection to that popular aromatic spice."

10. Humus explained, "This plant was so greatly respected by the Romans that it appeared in their art, literature, even architecture. They carried it wherever the Roman empire extended. Even to these, our British Isles. It was embraced by our hardy country folk, but shunned by the aristocracy. Still, if you are going to celebrate the Roman and Italian culture you must make this a part of your diet."

Dame Elizabeth cautiously brought the white bulb to her nose. Then she gasped, "Why this must be the most loved and hated of herbs. This must be . . . ."

In case you haven't identified this odorous bulb yet,
the answer is on page 123

From Ginger Rogers to Ginger Snaps

George and Blaine would often spend their afternoons, while others were playing Bingo sitting in the screenroom, discussing fondly remembered yesterdays, and even making up some good stories when reality wasn't enough. This afternoon they were waiting for the horticultural therapist to arrive for their weekly Green Thumb Club program. They had been told that they would be planting ginger.

George was thinking about Ginger Rogers and Fred Astaire. Blaine upstaged him when he mentioned that he had once met this movie star and actually gotten her autograph.

"She was beautiful, and a class act," Blaine commented.

George replied, "Yeah. Fred said she was a better dancer than he was 'cause he couldn't dance in high heels." They were both laughing over this when Becky, the horticultural therapist, arrived with several boxes of materials.

They helped her spread out all the stuff she had brought along. This included ginger ale, gingerbread cookies, ginger flowers and raw ginger.

"Got any movies of Fred & Ginger?" George asked as they spread the materials out on the tables.

"No." she said as she unpacked the bags and boxes and a crowd began to form around them. She had a growing ginger plant, a basket of ginger roots, a tray of gingerbread men, women & children, ginger snaps, ginger ale and a tea pot.

"I drank ginger tea when I was pregnant to keep the morning sickness away," one of the ladies said as she helped spread everything out on the table.

George laughed, "I had to drink it when I had a cold. Wasn't until years later I learned how much a little brandy improved it."

Becky passed around a copies of a little book called *Seniors Illustrated* that had a short story in it called *Gingerbread Friends*, while everyone found a seat around the table. "It's about an old lady and a bunch of kids getting together to bake gingerbread men, ladies and children for Christmas tree ornaments." Becky explained. "I thought you might want to try it this year."

You can have quite a Ginger Party, and everyone has memories of ginger in one of its many forms. You might even want to bake some gingerbread friends. Oh, if you have a DVD of one of Fred & Ginger's movies you might want to share it with your friends.

Just for Fun Ginger Quiz

Note: there may be more than one right answer.

1. Ginger Rogers and Fred Astaire made how many of those beautiful movies together?
a) 3,
b) 10,
c) 17,
d) 38

2. Ginger's given name was
a) Ginger
b) Ginel
c) Virginia
d) Joyce

3. There was another famous actress who played a character named Ginger in the TV series Gilligan's Island. Her given name is Tiatiana Blacker, but she is better known by her stage name
a) Natalie Schafer
b) Dawn Wells
c) Ida Lupino
d) Tina Louise

4. The Gilligan's Island character Ginger's last name is not well known, but perhaps you are a Ginger expert.
a) Grant
b) Williams
c) Astaire
d) Davis

5. Ginger snaps are often called what in Great Britain?
a) Ginger Wheels
b) Ginger Crackers
c) Ginger Nuts
d) Ginger Wafers

6. The fresh ginger you find in the produce department has a distinctive shape. These sections of ginger root are known by several names including
a) Toes
b) Horns
c) Bulbs
d) Antlers

7. Ginger pieces cooked with sugar will keep for a long time if stored properly. This delightful taste treat is called
a) Ginger drops
b) Candied ginger
c) Crystallized ginger
d) Dried ginger

8. Gingerbread cookies made in the shapes of people have become a popular Christmas tradition. Rumor has it that this playful custom was started by which British monarch?
a) Queen Victoria
b) King George III
c) Queen Elizabeth I
d) Henry VIII

9. Ginger has some spicy cousins including
a) Pepper
b) Turmeric
c) Garlic
d) Cardamom

10. John McLaughlin was a pharmacist in Toronto. He invented a special version of ginger ale called
a) Vernor's Real
b) Birchwood Ginger Ale
c) Ginger Champagne
d) Canada Dry

Answers:

1-b, 2-c, 3-d, 4-a, 5-c, 6-a, b & d, 7-b & c, 8-c, 9-b & d, 10-d.

Green Myths, Legends and Lies

In every corner of the world, in every culture, there are stories about the plants that surround us. Some of these are myths about the origin of certain species such as the Cherokee Rose that was said to have sprung from the tears shed by the Cherokee women as they lost children during the Trail of Tears. Some are legends to teach us valuable lessons, like the way Saint Patrick used the clover leaf to teach the Irish tribes about the Trinity. Some are true, and others are outright lies.

Sometimes the legends survive because we all long for good luck, or safety from lightning strikes or snake bites. We want to know the weather to come, and don't quite trust the weather forecaster on the evening news.

The few questions that follow are only the beginning. In your group there are most likely people from many different cultures. They are a rich resource for botanical myths, legends and lies. This quiz is best taken as a group effort, with open book and open mind. Let comments flow and encourage everyone to share their memories, their beliefs and their questions.

1. If tree leaves are turned upside down (some say inside out) this means
a) the wind is really strong
b) snow is on the way
c) the temperature will near 100°
d) it's going to rain

2. Picking a bouquet of pansies and bringing them indoors will bring
a) a frost
b) mosquitoes
c) cool weather
d) a gentle rain

3. Eating hazelnuts, so an old Irish legend goes, will
a) make you wise
b) make the object of your affections fall in love with you
c) bring gold
d) bring bad luck

4. The Native Americans of the American southwest often place a branch from a wolfberry shrub over their windows to
a) protect the home from illness
b) keep family members safe while on a journey
c) protect the family from lightning strikes
d) bring rain

5. In Europe it was said that when nightshade was made into a cream and rubbed all over a witch's body she
a) would be invisible
b) could fly
c) would talk with the devil
d) could go without eating for forty days

6. Ivy growing on the walls of an English home was thought to
a) draw snakes
b) keep the home warmer in winter
c) bring good luck
d) give shelter to the fairies

7. Which of the following is not thought to bring good luck?
a) cabbage
b) garlic
c) sage
d) tansy

8. The Scottish clans protected themselves from witches by carrying
a) a sprig of heather
b) a garlic bulb in the cap
c) a flask of whiskey
d) a thistle blossom

9. If a lady suffered from nightmares, what could be placed by her bed?
a) a bouquet of fern leaves
b) rosemary and lavender
c) a peony blossom
d) a spring of mistletoe

10. The wife rules the household where what grows well?
a) chives
b) rosemary
c) dandelions
d) red roses

11. If a child catches a falling leaf it is
a) a sign of good luck
b) protection from snake bites
c) proof of his, or her, frivolous nature
d) protection from catching a cold

12. A tree blooming out of season is thought to predict
a) a hard winter ahead
b) an approaching drought
c) a family feud or war within the next year
d) the death of a family member

13. Primroses were traditionally planted around the home to
a) encourage fairies
b) keep ants away
c) keep milk from spoiling
d) so that it could be used as a medicinal herb when needed

14. An old Turkish legend says that staring into the center of a poppy flower can
a) bring great wealth
b) cause memory loss
c) make you blind
d) bring the image of someone who loves you

15. A popular myth that continues even to today is that "to bloom, a peony plant needs . . ."
a) a companion peony plant,
b) ants,
c) a thunderstorm,
d) a robin's song

Answers:
1-d, 2-d, 3-a, 4-c, 5-b, 6-c, 7-b, 8-d, 9-c, 10-b.
11-d, 12-a, b, c, d, 13-a, 14-c, 15-b.

Holiday Flower and Plants

The end of the year is the season for celebrations, office parties and religious ceremonies. Christmas, Chanukah, Eid-Al-Adha, Bodhi Day, Kwanzaa and other holiday celebrations from other people and places seem to fall in the same season. This is an opportunity for us to learn a lot about each other, but it is also a great opportunity for us to share stories, help others become familiar with our own traditions, customs and ways of celebrating. Many of these holidays are expressed in art, music, literature, stories, decorations, gifts and, of course, food; often this is a feast.

In today's culture, directed by the marketplace, advertising, the internet and the TV, many of the traditions get lost in the shuffle. Some are transformed into something far distant from their origins. That's why the holidays are a great time of the year to bring children into the senior centers and elders into the schools.

This is a reverse quiz about holiday plants. Hopefully these will serve as springboards for discussion. We have given you the answers. All you have to do is create the questions, almost like Jeopardy. The following is an example:

The answers is: *The fig leaf*

The Question is: *What is reported to be our first clothing?*

We suggest that each creative participant make up 10 questions. What you do with them is also up to you. Have fun.

Apple	Jerusalem Cherry
Amaryllis	Kalanchoe
Azalea	Mistletoe
Christmas cactus	Norfolk Island Pine
Dates	Orange
Hellabores, Christmas rose	Pine
Chrysanthemum	Poinsettia
Cyclamen	Rose
Figs	Rosemary
Fir	Spruce
Holly	Yew
Ivy	

Chocolate in the Garden of Delights

What is the meaning of life?
All evidence to date suggests it's chocolate.

Chances are you are not growing a chocolate tree on your windowsill, but it is still one of the most intriguing of this planet's botanical treasures. This native of the American tropics has changed the way people live all over the world. It has been feared as a "devil's drug" and revered as the "food of the gods." It is respected as a health food, viewed in some circles as an aphrodisiac, considered a cheap anti-depressant, an energy booster and a mood enhancer. The cocoa bean is above all else a valuable global agricultural and economic commodity.

Chocolate doesn't make the world go 'round,
but it sure does make the trip worthwhile!

Wise people have made sometimes profound comments about chocolate in its various forms. Thomas Jefferson wrote in his journal, *"The superiority of chocolate, both for health and nourishment, will soon give it the same preference over tea and coffee in America which it has in Spain."*

Perhaps he was inspired by an old Spanish proverb *"Las cosas claras y el chocolate espeso. (Ideas should be clear and chocolate thick.)"*

If they don't have chocolate in heaven, I ain't going.

Even an authority of no less stature than Homer Simpson (now honored on a US postage stamp), in the language of diplomacy stated, *"Let us celebrate our agreement with the adding of chocolate to milk."*

Save the Earth! It's the only planet with chocolate.

Chocolate has been ridiculed and revered, but, regardless of how you personally feel about this botanical delight, it does make us smile. We all know jokes about chocolate. Some may be in poor taste (this doesn't always negate the humor in the joke) but many are based on basic truths.

The ability of chocolate to calm, soothe, relieve depression and improve your sense of well being is common knowledge. This is Dave Barry's take on that.

My therapist told me the way to achieve true inner peace is to finish what I start. So far today, I have finished 2 bags of M&M's and a chocolate cake. I feel better already.

Others have made similar observations, such as;.

Chocolate is cheaper than therapy and you don't need an appointment.

And

Chocolate isn't a food, it's a medicine - an anti-depressant.

Chocolate has long been associated with sex and respected as an aphrodisiac. This actually began with the Aztecs and the Spanish conquistadores where 10 cocoa beans was the going price for the companionship of a prostitute.

Twill make Old Women Young and Fresh; Create New Motions of the Flesh. And cause them to long for you know what, if they but taste of chocolate. - James Wadsworth, A History of the Nature and Quality of Chocolate

A man found a bottle on the beach. He opened it and out popped a genie, who gave the man three wishes. The man wished for a million dollars, and poof! There was a million dollars. Then he wished for a convertible, and poof! There was a convertible. And then, he wished he could be irresistible to all women... Poof! He turned into a box of chocolates.

I have this theory that chocolate slows down the aging process.... It may not be true, but do I dare take the chance?

When we were doing a chocolate tasting at an assisted living center, one of the residents shard the following story, proving that we are never too old for chocolate.

An elderly man lay dying in his bed.
In death's agony, he suddenly smelled the aroma of his favorite chocolate chip cookies wafting up the stairs.
Gathering his remaining strength, he lifted himself from the bed. He slowly made his way out of the bedroom, and, with even greater effort, forced himself down the stairs, gripping the railing with both hands. With labored breath, he leaned against the door, gazing into the kitchen.
Were it not for death's agony, he would have thought himself already in heaven: there, spread out on the kitchen table, were hundreds of his favorite chocolate chip cookies.
Mustering one final effort, he threw himself toward the table. His aged and withered hand painstakingly made its way toward a cookie when it was suddenly smacked by a spatula.
"Stay out of those," said his wife, "they're for the funeral."

Some final chocolate thoughts and smiles.

Put a smile on your face,
make the world a better place.
from an old Hershey's Chocolate advertisement

As a writer I have to agree with the following

Chocolate is a perfect food, as wholesome as it is delicious,
a beneficent restorer of exhausted power.
It is the best friend of those engaged in literary pursuits.
--Baron Justus von Liebig (1803-1873) German chemist

Chocolate Candy Quiz, part one

It seems that everyone has fond memories of many chocolate products. Manufacturers have been promoting various chocolate candy bars, snacks and assorted treats through the years. They have produced many memorable advertisements, slogans and jingles. The following is only the beginning. Can you match the candy bar with the slogans in the following? Let's see which of these are memorable and which ones have been forgotten. In one group, each of those participating voted on their three favorite chocolate bars and their three most memorable slogans.

1. ___ "Melts in your mouth, not in your hand."

2. ___ "The great American chocolate bar."

3. ___ "Sometimes you feel like a nut. Sometimes you don't."

4. ___ "Hungry? Why wait?"

5. ___ "Gimme a break"

6. ___ "Crispety, crunchety, peanut-buttery"

7. ___ "Two for me, none for you."

8. ___ "At work, rest and play, you get three great tastes in a _____ _____"

9. ___ "Get the sensation"

10.___ "For the kid in you"

A. Nestle's Crunch

B. Butterfinger

C. Twix

D. York Peppermint Patty

E. Almond Joy & Mounds

F. Hershey's

G. Milky Way

H. Kit Kat

I. M & M's

J. Snickers

Chocolate Candy Quiz, part two

1. The Necco Candy Company launched a unique candy bar in 1938 with a sky writing ad campaign. This candy bar is unique because it contains four distinct flavors. Necco's aerial ads were for the

a) Chocolate only Wafers

b) Sky Bar

c) Grand Bar

d) O Henry

2. The Curtiss Candy Company promoted its popular candy bar by dropping thousands from a plane over Pittsburgh. Each candy bar had a tiny parachute attached.

a) O Henry

b) Zagnut

c) Baby Ruth

d) Steel City Bar

3. In a series of TV commercials, various animals including camels and kangaroos made a request. They all said, "I want a . . . ."

a) Hershey Bar

b) Milky Way

c) Mounds

d) Clark Bar

4. One popular ad campaign claimed, "There's no wrong way to eat a . . . . ."
a) Reese's Peanut Butter Cup

b) Tootsie Roll

c) Zero Bar

d) Kit Kat Bar

5. "It's more than a mouthful– it's . . . ."
a) O Henry

b) Baby Ruth

c) Whatchamacallit!

d) Dynamite Bar

6. In the 70's the question was "Where do you hide to have your . . . . .?"
a) Heath Bar

b) Snickers

c) Butterfinger

d) Pay Day

7. The most popular chocolate bar in America in 2008 was
a) Butterfinger

b) Snickers

c) Reese's

d) Hershey Bar

8. "All I really need is love, but a little chocolate now and then doesn't hurt!" is a memorable quote from which cartoon character?
a) Lois Lane

b) Brenda Star

c) Little Orphan Annie

d) Lucy Van Pelt, Peanuts

9. "And above all... Think Chocolate!" was the opinion expressed by
a) Betty Crocker
b) Julia Childe
c) Emerile
d) The Iron Chef

10. The famous quote, "Momma always said life is like a box of chocolates. You never know what you're gonna get." Was spoken by . . . .
a) Russell Stover
b) Mark Twain
c) Ronald Reagan
d) Forrest Gump

Chocolate Bubble Bath

This recipe was shared with us by an 83 year old lady who said that it gave her a healthy attitude and smooth, sexy skin. She claimed that it was a matter of the soothing creamy texture of the bath as well as the subtle chocolate fragrance. She explained that when she was depressed by the evening news, angry with the TV ads or the arthritis was a bother, this was her solution.

What you need to prepare for this decadent indulgence:

1 dark chocolate Hershey bar (any dark chocolate will work, about 2 to 4 ounces)

A vegetable grater to turn the chocolate bar into very small pieces

1/3 to 1/2 cup of soy milk

1 bottle of unscented bubble bath

a good book to read while relaxing in the tub (optional)

some soothing music to play in the background. Caution: keep radio, CD player or other means of music production away from the bath water

Putting it all together:

1. Grate the dark chocolate. The finer the better.

2. Heat the soy milk in a sauce pan, or double boiler at a low heat, stirring frequently to prevent scorching. Do not let it begin to boil. (Some use a microwave for this step.)

3. Add the grated chocolate to the heated soy milk. Continue stirring until the chocolate is completely melted.

4. Allow this "hot chocolate" to cool while you gather a towel, book and music.

5. Begin filling the tub with warm water, a temperature you are comfortable with. (Not too hot for diabetics.)

6. Add sufficient bubble bath to form lots of bubbles and stir in the "hot chocolate."

7. Inhale deeply, step into your chocolate bath and relax, enjoy the book and the music.

Squirrels on Parade

If you grew up in the country, you probably got to gather walnuts, hazelnuts, pecans, hickory nuts or some other local harvest. This was a race with the squirrels, and it ain't as easy to outsmart one of them as you might think. Nutting was usually done in the fall when it was cold, damp and generally unpleasant to be outside, unless we were playing football. Dad joked that we looked like a bunch of squirrels on parade as we ran around picking up the fallen nuts. But collecting the darn things was the easy part. They had to be husked, shelled, etc. City kids missed all this fun.

One of the old timers at the senior center in Monaca, PA told us this little story. "The black walnuts were the worst. They had that green outer shell that contained a very aromatic dark tannic acid that stained your clothes and hands almost black. Have to admit that sometimes we used it like war paint. We convinced Jimmy that you had to take your shoes off and dance on the walnuts in their husks to set the nuts free. It took him a while to notice that we still had our shoes on. Once Jimmy fell asleep and we squeezed the juice all over his face and turned his blonde hair awful dark in spots. Don't think his folks ever forgave us for that."

Andy stroked what was left of his hair and added, "After that you had to crack them. Rare was the kid in school without battered fingers from using a hammer, or brick or heavy stone in this process."

Nora actually took us out on the remote reaches of the Acoma Pueblo reservation in New Mexico to gather pinons, or pinon nuts. These are the seeds of a pine tree, the *Pinus edulis*. They have a delightful flavor when salted and roasted. She was kind enough to teach us how to collect, prepare and eat this autumn treat. In every group there are people just waiting to tell their stories. Others have stories to tell but are shy or insecure. By starting with this little quiz, discussions can be ignited and perhaps even a story or two will be shared. If some of these nuts can be brought in for the group, recipes discussed and favorites voted on, a whole lot of informal interaction can just happen. Have fun with the little quiz. Don't take it too seriously, let go and enjoy.

107

A Nuttin' We Will Go, the quiz

Nuts have always been one of the basic foods for people everywhere throughout the history of human existence. They are very nutritious, store easily and keep for a long time. Let's explore some of these with a few 'nutty' questions. Who knows, might even spark a few memories for you.   If the memories aren't good enough, you can even make up a couple stories.

1. The native American butternut was used to dye the uniforms of the Confederate soldiers during the Civil War. This small tree is related to

a) The Buckeye

b) Black Walnut

c) Hazelnut

d) Macadamia nut

2. Copra is dried

a) Acorn meal

b) Ground peanuts

c) Coconut meat

d) Water chestnuts

3. Which of these grows underground?

a) Cashews

b) Corn nuts

c) Peanuts

d) Pistachios

4. Which of these nuts does not come from the tropics?

a) Coconuts

b) Filberts

c) Brazil nuts

d) Cashews

5. Pignolia nuts are the seeds of

a) immature pecans

b) pine cones

c) the pig palm

d) apricots

6. The litchi nut is the seed of the _____ fruit
a) Farkleberry
b) Date palm
c) Lychee
d) Jujube

7. Macadamia nuts are native to
a) Central Africa
b) Germany & Eastern Europe
c) China
d) Israel

8. American chestnuts are virtually extinct because
a) a virus killed all the trees
b) there was such high demand for the wood that all the trees were logged
c) it is impossible to domesticate them
d) Japanese beetles devoured the leaves of young trees

9. The almond is most closely related to
a) apples
b) maples
c) oaks
d) peaches

10. English walnuts originally grew in
a) China
b) Scotland
c) The Carpathian Mountains
d) South Africa

11. The Hazelnut is also known as
a) Filbert
b) Kumquat
c) Kola nut
d) Horsechestnut

12. Of the following native American nuts, which one is poisonous?
a) Butternut
b) Black walnut
c) Horsechestnut
d) Pinon pine

13. Which of the following is not grown on trees?
a) Cashews
b) Macadamia nuts
c) Corn Nuts
d) Pistachio nuts

14. Which of the following is related to poison ivy?
a) Almonds
b) Beer nuts
c) Water chestnuts
d) Cashews

15. What is the most popular nut in the United States?
a) Black walnuts
b) Peanuts
c) Almonds
d) Pecans

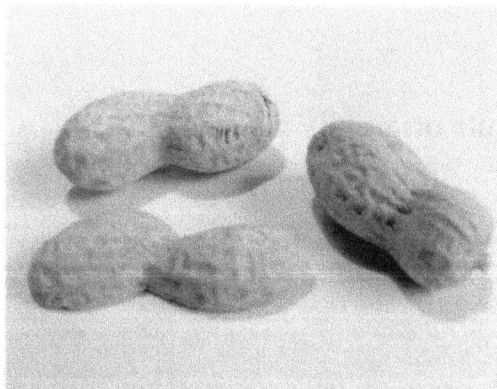

It's a Zoo Out There

Racine and Jerry were both retired teachers. But, teachers are a lot like Marines. You know the saying "Once a Marine always a Marine." Well, once a teacher, always a teacher. They were both residents of the Birchwood Falls Assisted Living Community, but they spent a lot of time looking over the fence at the playground of the Birchwood Elementary School next door.

At their urging, the activity director arranged for an "intergenerational encounter." About a dozen third graders were brought over after school for a brief visit. It was a little awkward at first, but Racine and Jerry soon took over and gave them a grand tour, including the little garden behind the apartments.

"What kinda flower's that?" a little girl asked, pointing to the white flowers on a tree by the strolling path. "A dogwood," Jerry answered.

Soon they were pointing out various plants, asking a few questions and telling a couple stories. They also listened as the children related some of their favorites and even sang *The Garden Song* made popular by John Denver and The Muppets. You know, "Inch by inch, row by row . . ."

They were introduced to foxgloves and pussy willows, ostrich ferns and tiger lilies. One shy and quiet child knelt down and touched the petals of a dogtooth violet. "Wish we could plant a garden like this at school," he said. Then he looked up at Racine with a smile. "Ma'am, you got a flower zoo here." That's the comment that started it all.

It took a few weeks to get all the authorities on board for the project. In that length of time there were several visits back and forth between the school and the "old folks." They started making a list of all the plants with animal names that they could grow in their Zoo Garden.

"I want skunk cabbage," one of the children shouted. Everyone laughed but later Jerry took a field trip and returned with two plastic bags full of this foul smelling swamp plant. They were planted beside the cattails.

111

Now they need your help. Reach back into the deep dark recesses of your mind and see what "zoo plants" you can come up with. If that doesn't work, do some research. Study the seed and nursery catalogs, use the internet, take a field trip to a local garden center, ask the residents of a senior community or the visitors to a senior meals site. Work with the students in a local school, after all it will be their garden too. Once you have a good list, everyone in the community can work together to make it a reality.

You can use the following for your list, or you can design your own. You can work alone, but it's more fun if it's a group effort.

It's up to you what to plant in your botanical zoo

Jerry decided to get everyone involved in art for the garden. They all made plaques with the plant name and a sketch of the animal. Some of these were quite involved, others were somewhat more abstract. He had them do theirs on cheap ceramic tiles, but you can use any medium you choose.

Racine started the kids off with a garden journal where everything from drawings and poetry to planting notes was recorded.

Several folks at the Birchwood Falls Assisted Living Community took photos of the planning, preparation, planting and growth of the "Flower Zoo." Several of the students posted pictures, comments and some of their poetry on the school's web site.

You can do this with house plants too, and make an indoor Flower Zoo. Of course there are such ominous ones as spider plant and snake plant. But many are not quite as common, like the peacock ferns and burro's tails.

Other themes besides animals can be used. In various projects around the United States many great ideas have become gardens. One group made a Global Garden of plants with names of countries or geographical locations. Another made theirs a botanical journey through history and listed plants with famous people's names; while another compiled a list of people with plant names. They included Daisy Duck and Olive Oyl (Popeye's girlfriend).

It's a Zoo Out There, Just for Fun Quiz

Set your mind free and get out of the way. You never know what might happen. Can you match these residents of the botanical zoo?

1   +   = _____

2   +   = _____

3   +   = _____

4   +   = _____

5   +   = _____

6   +   = _____

Answers on page 123

Ideas for the Floral Zoo

Trees and shrubs with animal names

_____
_____
_____
_____
_____

Flowers, bulbs, herbs and other plants hardy for your area

_____
_____
_____
_____
_____
_____
_____
_____
_____

Weeds that might growl, tweet, bark, purr or chirp

_____
_____
_____
_____
_____
_____
_____

Special Stuff

_____
_____
_____

Friendship Plants, a Treasure Hunt Game

In the good old days:

It was once the custom, back in the Good Old Days, to share snips and sprigs of plants with family, friends, guests and casual visitors. It was usually something that grew easily from a cutting. This was a token of friendship and a way of sharing. It was also a way, in days that were perhaps a little less commercial, to obtain something new and different. Sometimes it was something commonplace, sometimes it was a rare, almost one of a kind plant that had been in the family for generations. Often the official names of these plants were lost through the years that it had been a botanical family pet. They were often given names that seemed appropriate to the owners.

Sometimes these friendship plants were only cuttings shared, other times Mama or Grandma had little plants started in old tin cans. Sometimes this was a project for the kids on a rainy day. The idea was to share a living plant as a symbol of friendship. It's possible to populate your entire windowsill with such shared plants, tokens of friendship, a living scrapbook of acquaintances, or a botanical journey down memory lane. The following is a "just for fun" project for gardeners of all ages, designed to promote friendship and re-discover a great tradition from the past. We strongly recommend this as an intergenerational game.

There are three parts to this indoor Treasure Hunt

Part 1, Great plants I have grown

Begin by making a list of ten plants that bring a smile when you think about them. You can write a sentence or two about each of the plants on your list if you wish. Perhaps just a few words that explain why you chose this plant. The plants on the next page are only suggestions. Each of us have favorites that someone we knew had on their windowsill, or perhaps shared with us when we were a child.

Once you have your list, you can start the quest. Contact friends and family members. See if they are still growing one or more of the plants on your Top Ten list. If they are, ask them to bring, or send, seeds, cuttings or young plants to you. *One basic rule: none of these plants can be bought.* You don't have to collect all ten plants, try for about three different ones.

Some Friendship Plant Suggestions

African violets

Aluminum Plant

Angel Wing Begonia

Basil, many varieties start from cuttings

Begonias, many colors, shapes and leaf forms

Boston Fern, started from divisions

Bridal Veil

Christmas Cactus

Coleus

English ivy

Geraniums, a multitude of varieties

Hens & Chicks

Hoya, Wax Plant

Inch plant

Jade Plant

Kalanchoes, flowering types

Maternity plant, Mother of Many

Peace lily

Pepperomia

Philodendron, many types

Purple passion plant

Rabbit's Foot Fern

Sansevieria, Snake Plant

Swedish ivy

Spider plant

Wandering Jew

Zig-Zag cactus, also called Ric-Rac cactus

Your favorites that will make good friendship plants:

_____

_____

_____

_____

_____

_____

_____

_____

_____

_____

_____

_____

_____

Again, these are only suggestions. There are hundreds of old familiar friends that aren't mentioned here.

My Top Ten List:

1._____

Comments:_____
_____
_____

2._____

Comments:_____
_____
_____

3._____

Comments:_____
_____
_____

4._____

Comments:_____
_____
_____

5._____

Comments:_____
_____
_____

6._____

Comments:_____
_____

7._____

Comments:_____
_____

8._____

Comments:_____
_____
_____

9._____

Comments:_____
_____
_____

10._____

Comments:_____
_____
_____

Part 2: The treasure hunt continues.

While you are waiting for the plants to arrive, you can begin the quest for something to plant them in. The more outrageous the better. You can go through the closets or kitchen cabinets, visit a local thrift store or a yard sale. We have seen creative folks use everything from old shoes to a broken Jack-in-the-Box, tomato soup cans to coffee mugs, candy tins to an old purse. In the book *Windowsill Whimsy, Gardening & Horticultural Therapy Projects for Small Spaces* by the authors of this book, there are numerous projects involving unique, novel, light-hearted, creative and found containers. These are an opportunity to liberate the artist within. It's OK to trade great finds. You can even work as teams if you wish.

After you have found the treasure that will serve as the "perfect" pot for your friendship plant, it's time to decorate it. This is another treasure hunt. Go to the junk drawer, the craft supplies corner, or go through whatever decorative materials you have stashed away. These can be items to glue onto the container, or simply stick in the soil as a whimsy. Be creative. Use paint, stickers, ribbon, silk flowers, buttons, whatever treasures you can find.

Part 3: Time for another list.

This is the most important quest for this little treasure hunt. Now you can make a list of people you would like to give the gift of a smile, or perhaps, someone you would like to have as a new friend.

You aren't on this treasure hunt to find some old, long forgotten plant. The objective isn't to find a lighthearted container, or the stuff to decorate it with. The real treasure is friendship, both rediscovered old friends and new found friends never met before. That's why these gifts are called Friendship Plants. You can even be creative and design a gift card to go with the plant.

These were sometimes called pass-along plants. This can be done with both indoor and outdoor plants. Enjoy the gift of giving, of sharing your memories, your smiles and your plants.

In the Garden of My Dreams

This is the final little project in this book. This is not a test. It is a look at tomorrow. Gardeners are rich in memories. We can close our eyes and taste the unbeatable flavor of a ripe tomato picked from the vine on a hot summer afternoon years ago. But gardeners don't live in yesterday. We are always looking forward to tomorrow.

With every seed sown, every bulb planted we can see the leaves and the flowers to come. When we tend our garden, even if it is only a potted friend on the windowsill, we inhale hope and anticipation.

The gardener is always able to look for the surprise; and the gardener is always waiting for tomorrow, because that's where the next flower blooms, where the next harvest will be found. But the garden isn't only a place where plants grow. The garden is where the gardener grows as well. In fact the garden is far more about the people than the plants. The gardener blooms with smiles at the scent of the herbs, the colors of the flowers, the texture of the tulip leaf, the sound of the birds singing with us, the taste of fresh mint, and the comfort that comes from being with the earth itself.

The garden is our connection to reality in a virtual world. We can explore, discover, relax, communicate without words with a creator who speaks all languages. We are free to meditate, contemplate, remember and anticipate when we are in the company of our green friends. The garden doesn't judge, scold or criticize us. It welcomes us as we are, with faulty memories, arthritic hands, aching backs or clouded eyes.

Not only is the garden a friend, it is a comfortable place to share with friends. The garden is the place of dreams and hopes. In the garden we can share the wonder of life, the joy of being alive, the smile of the moment. In the garden we are empowered, inspired, invigorated and comforted. The future lives in the garden. Tomorrow blooms there, and so can we. Much is written and spoken about reminisce and memory gardens. But the garden is a living thing, and as gardeners we are a part of it. We too are alive in the garden. We cannot be passive in the companionship of plants. We cannot help but be engaged and enlivened.

In the gardening experience, we get to make choices. We get to choose our friends, both those we plant in the garden and those who will stroll with us on this incredible journey we call life.

The following are some questions that you can answer if you wish. This is your decision. You can share the queries and the answers with friends. You can make this a family activity, or a group experience. This too, is your decision.

In my garden I would like to grow

List five or ten plants that you would like to grow; perhaps something like a red geranium that calls forth fond memories, or an orchid you have never tried growing before. You can look through magazines, catalogs, web sites or botanical gardens for ideas. No two people will have the same list, because we each come at life from a unique perspective. We each have our own set of experiences and memories, hopes and fears, dreams and nightmares. We all carry emotional scars that sometimes make us stronger, and sometimes limit us. On this page describe your dream garden (even if it is on a windowsill) and think about why you are making these selections.

1.

2.

3.

4.

5.

> We can grow much more than flowers and plants in our gardens. We can grow food, hope, self confidence, friends and children. For many, faith also grows in the garden. Sometimes these are accidental blossoms. One of our green thumb club members calls this "a wild harvest of joy." Every day gives you little garden surprises; all you have to do is look for them. Then you have the opportunity to share your discoveries.

How I would describe my dream garden:

_____

_____

_____

_____

_____

If I could give my dream garden a name I would call it

_____

_____

Special friends I would invite to share my garden include

_____

_____

_____

_____

_____

How I would like to have visitors describe my garden

_____

_____

_____

_____

_____

Answers to the Sherlock Humus mini-mysteries

Page 17-18. Sherlock Humus and the case of the Mysterious Blooming House Plant. The answer is **African violet**

> One elderly friend always had a windowsill jammed full of little African violets she had started from the leaves. Visitors, door-to-door sales people, even strangers who had lost their way never left her home without one of these little "friendship plants" and a little poem she had written that told how to care for it.

page 23-24. Sherlock Humus and the Mysterious Case of Death with a Smile.

The answer is **chocolate**.

> Columbus introduced chocolate to Europe but after months at sea, the beans were spoiled and moldy. They added another spice brought back from the Americas, hot peppers called chiles to the steaming drink they called hot chocolate. It wasn't very popular for almost a century. Then they learned how to dry the chocolate before setting sail.
>
> Chocolate consumption has been scientifically linked to longer life. A few pieces of chocolate every month may make your life both sweeter and longer, according to the Harvard School of Public Health. Chocolate beans and pods were used as money by residents of some Central American countries as late as the 1800's.

page 41-42. Sherlock Humus and the Case of the April Fool's Day Flower. The answer is the **dandelion**.

> This much despised little wild flower has been the universal toy of childhood, the source of nutritious greens, the main ingredient in a traditional wine and a symbol of courage and tenacity in the face of adversity.
>
> In some of our Green Thumb Clubs the members have compiled lists of ways to use various parts of the dandelion plant, created artworks and written poems about it, and even taught visiting children how to make a dandelion whistle, a dandelion chain, and even dandelion flower ice cream.

Page 53-54. Sherlock Humus and the case of the Purloined Flowers. The stolen flowers were, you're right, **lilacs.**

Lilacs haunt our memories and ignite our senses. This shrub appears in the poetry of Whitman and the writing of Louis May Alcott and many others.

Gather lilacs, inhale their fragrance and share delightful memories. It's even better if these memories are shared while barefoot in the grass. Perhaps even while blowing bubbles and delighting in play.

Did you ever make a flute from a lilac twig? Try it.

Sharing yesterday is great, but making new memories today is even better.

Page 88-90. Sherlock Humus and case of the Mysterious Odor. And the answer is **garlic.**

Garlic has more medicinal uses, appears in more recipes and is the star in more myths, legends and stories that any other plant. It has a fascinating history, from being the basic method of payment for the laborers building the Egyptian pyramids to being used as an effective antiseptic during many wars including WWI and WWII. Everyone knows their share of garlic stories and this is a great topic for discussion. One of our green thumb clubs even wrote a little book about garlic.

Answers to It's a Zoo Out There page 113
1. Crabgrass, 2. Dogwood, 3. Tiger lily, 4. Skunk cabbage, 5. Cattails, 6. Hen & Chicks

Petals & Pages Press introduces
SENIORS ILLUSTRATED
a new series for Mature Readers

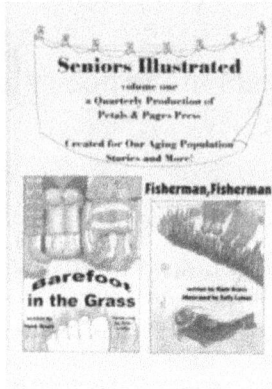

Petals & Pages Press is pleased to announce a new series of books for our mature populations. *Seniors Illustrated* was inspired by and created for our elders, both at home and in senior care communities. These are short stories with older adults as the heroes and heroines. There will be four new titles released per year. Each is written to respect and honor our elders, but can be enjoyed by all ages.

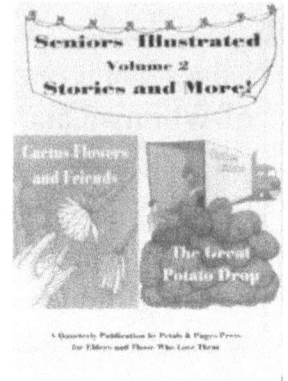

Why did we create Seniors Illustrated?

It all started when we were doing a horticultural therapy training program for the staff at a senior care community last year. As we entered the activities room we noticed a stack of Little Golden Books on the table. You know, those little children's books with the children's stories and lots of pictures. After our program we complimented the activity director on their intergenerational program. She said, "Oh, we don't have an intergenerational program. Why did you think we did?"

We pointed to the Little Golden Books on the table and started to explain that we assumed the elders living there were reading them to the children who visited.

She responded, "That's all we could find for many of our seniors who have trouble following the plot in a novel, or even holding a big book in arthritic hands." She then spread some of the books out on the table. "This is the best we could do."

We contacted a number of our friends involved in senior care, rehab programs and hospitals. They all decried the lack of reading material written and formatted for senior citizens. Others agreed that they had attempted to provide opportunities to read by supplying children's picture books. This is minimally effective at best. The characters and plots don't speak to the interests of senior citizens. The presentation doesn't provide the mental stimulation that can be most beneficial for persons with cognitive impairments and memory limitations.

To remedy this situation, we launched a series of senior short story / picture books written specifically for elders. Seniors Illustrated stories are written and illustrated to entertain, amuse, inspire and engage mature readers, including those with physical and mental limitations. Subject matter varies from senior romance to elder heroes making a difference in the world, poetry for inspiration and conversation, a little humor and a few activities.

What does a Seniors Illustrated book look like?

Each title will be paperback, about 60 to 70 pages in an easy to hold 8 ½ x 11 format, with a glossy cover. This size is convenient for arthritic hands. They will have full page illustrations on the left page and accompanying text on the facing page. This gives the visual impact first, followed by the words in large print. There will be more white space than is commonly found in adult literature. This makes it easier to focus and read with impaired vision, or cognitive limitations. The pictures are black & white outline form so that individual readers can color them if they so desire. This can reinforce the story by expanding the visual and verbal information to include physical input. The act of coloring makes the reader a partner in the story. It also provides readers the opportunity to make their own interpretations and decisions, another empowering activity. Many have chosen to add details or background as an outlet for their creativity.

Poetry is a part of each Senior's Illustrated book. The format and rhyme of a poem is often a great memory trigger and many individuals with cognitive impairment can interpret lines of a poem better than prose.

Seniors Illustrated Book Club

These stories are designed to be shared with family members, friends or activity groups. They can serve as the starting point for conversation, and many outline activities and mental exercises, discussion topics and opportunities for community involvement. We are encouraging the formation of a **Seniors Illustrated Book Club** where family, friends and neighbors can meet and discuss the Seniors Illustrated stories, share their own memories, ideas and dreams.

Some senior communities have started a reading club that meets periodically to share literary discussion, open conversation and find enjoyment. If you don't already have a book or reading club, why not start one? The stories in this Seniors Illustrated series can be read individually, or aloud to the group. Take the opportunity to discuss the book, share your thoughts and memories. But, most of all enjoy a good story, either one you read or one you tell.

Comments by Kathryn Martin on Seniors Illustrated Vol. 1
Oct 23, 2009

Kathryn Martin is a speaker, humorist, author and she plays Miz Maudie across the country. She has devoted her life to enriching the lives of America's elders and giving the gift of laughter to everyone. Her website www.mizmaudie.com provides insight into her diverse talents. She had the following comments to make after reading Seniors Illustrated Vol. 1. This is what she had to say.

The package arrived just as I was leaving.... so quickly opened it for a quick glance... Very attractive!!!! The book is so good, I never quit until I'd read the entire thing!!!

I find the book very attractive.

Front Cover: Shiny but not too shiny to create a glare for older eyes. FEELS good to the touch. Has a comforting feeling and size for arthritic hands to hold easily.

Inside: Print just right. Good quality paper... no glare to read...yet will accept coloring...

These are two stories that are impossible to put down without finishing! You've captured the essence without wasted words...Just easy enjoyable reading.. sense of anticipation... a little nervousness that the main characters will get caught.... the joy at seeing the "bad guys" put in their places.... then realizing how far they've been missing the mark... changing.... wonderful!!! I am really impressed.

Tomi's work is just woven into the whole thing so wonderfully. What a good idea to include something like that as so many of the older folks have enjoyed memorizing poems in their earlier years...lots of recitation... so still enjoy good poetry.

Sally's art work is really custom made.... It's easy to look at... has enough detail to back up the story ... gives one a picture of the characters and locale... yet simple and easy to color.

Then to put in suggested activities .. fantastic ideas.

I'd say from here, **"You've got a hit on your hands!"**

Kathryn

www.ingramcontent.com/pod-product-compliance
Lightning Source LLC
Chambersburg PA
CBHW081233090426
42738CB00016B/3284